MHMorris Co.

STRATEGIC PLANNING
FOR THE SMALL BUSINESS

STRATEGIC PLANNING

FOR THE SMALL BUSINESS

Situations, Weapons, Objectives & Tactics

Craig S. Rice

BOB ADAMS, INC.
PUBLISHERS

Holbrook, Massachusetts

Published by Bob Adams, Inc.
260 Center Street, Holbrook, MA 02343

ISBN: 1-55850-858-9

Printed in the United States of America

1   2   3   4   5   6   7   8   9   10

This publication is designed to provide accurate and authoritative information with regard to the subject matter covered. It is sold with the understanding that the publisher is not engaged in rendering legal, accounting, or other professional advice. If legal advice or other expert assistance is required, the services of a qualified professional person should be sought.

—From *A Declaration of Principles* jointly adopted by a Committee of the American Bar Association and a Committee of Publishers and Associations.

Table of Contents

1

Your Competitive Advantage

Responsibility gravitates to those who can.

— Drucker

Welcome! And Congratulations to you! The moment you opened this book, you jumped ahead of many of your competitors—because you are thinking about planning. Most firms rarely do this, and many don't even know the meaning of the word. But the world's best companies do.

You'll find this book is user-friendly. Most chapters are short. Each is divided into three parts.

First an idea is explained.

Second, this idea is demonstrated.

Then, *third,* you can do it yourself with a practical project form.

Plain English is spoken here. We use mostly familiar words and short sentences. These pages won't try to snow you with jibberish, jargon,or techno-babble. We respect you too much for that. We treat you like a real, live, important person, not some nameless audience. We talk with you, not at you—and we talk in terms of your interests. In fact you'll notice that is just exactly what we do; we talk, we don't lecture. We talk to you as a friend. We are also mindful that your time is valuable, so we get right to the point. We try to stay simple, easy, and interesting while never forgetting our purpose—to make more money for you.

You also get twelve exclusives that are provided in no other plans book:

1. A feasibility self-test system to see if your plan will work. This builds your confidence and impresses investors.

2. Separate, specific plans for six departments, marketing, production, finance, inside staff, outside helpers, and the group that sells the plan. Other books don't have this.

3. A general strategy for each department under nine different situations they might face.

4. Seven success examples that you can imitate. Each illustrates a different type of plan.

5. An equal balance of discussion, examples and forms to use.

6. Ideas on how to sell your business plan, even to especially tough people, such as bankers, owners, doubters, and others.

7. Ideas on how to train a planner: information that saves time.

8. A motivation plan to enthuse your team.

9. A time management plan to get more results per day.

10. Tested, proven plans. Each plan writer actually did this successfully and, as a professional authority, taught it to others.

11. Export plans designed for the booming 1990s in Europe, Asia, and elsewhere. No other plan book has this.

12. Ideas on how to make quick corrections as conditions change.

You may be wondering, "What does a business plan do for me?"

You are asking a sensible question that deserves an answer.

You get six strong benefits.

First *A plan favorably impresses your key people.* Your investors, owners, bankers, and employees often will say, "I like a person who has a good plan worked out!" Investors are more willing to put in funds — and employees will invest more of their time, effort, and enthusiasm. Programs motivate, and a person with a careful plan often has a certain attraction and influence.

Second *A plan increases your income.* Famous consultant Peter Drucker says, "What gets planned, gets done." So if you build a good, sensible program for increasing your sales and profits, you have a much better chance that those profits will come to you than you would if you had no such plan.

Third *A plan saves you time, work, and stress — and that's not all bad.* You avoid wasted action, mistakes, and lost money. The plan spreads and delegates the load. (Why should you do it all?) Plus, a plan anticipates problems and turns them into advantages before they hit you. So it cuts your stress. Good planners get more fun out of life.

Fourth *A plan applies your strengths, skills, abilities, interests.* Everyone and every company has talents. Yet these are sometimes unrecognized, unappreciated, and under-employed, even though these very things are the activities that people most enjoy doing, and often will generate the most results per day or week. A good plan helps find those valuable resources and applies them in constructive ways—like making money.

Fifth *A plan gives you a track to run on.* A railroad train, racing car, or running athlete moves better, more efficiently, more effectively, when on a track. All can see where they are, where they are going, and the direction they want to take. And a track is usually smoother than fields, streams, and woods. Your route is well laid out. Now you can concentrate on your own progress, speed, excelling over competitors and winning, rather than getting past every aggravating puddle, rock, and rut in the road.

Sixth *A plan sets priorities.* This can be very important and mighty handy in these days of limited resources and modest budgets. We simply can't afford to do everything. Some things must be postponed.

But other projects are essential. And even among these preferred projects, not everything can be done at once. With a plan, you know what to do first and what's coming next. It not only saves you from unpleasant surprises, but lets you focus all your skill on each step, so you are more likely to succeed. And by taking things one at a time, not in one horrendous load, your stress factor is much lower. Life is hard, by the yard—but life's a cinch, by the inch.

Who should read this book? Anyone who wants to use available resources to get maximum profit. Anyone who wants to avoid costly mistakes. This is generally one or several of these ten: a top manager, an owner, a partner, a vice-president, a consultant, a major lender or shareholder, a professional planner, an instructor, or a person new to planning. In short, anyone who wants a clear insight into the process will benefit from reading this book.

Part I

The Basics

2

What Do We Mean by a Strategic Plan?

Reach for the stars. At least you won't end up with a hand full of dirt.
— Leo Burnett

Simply put, a strategic plan is a program or way to manage resources to get profits. A good program or plan even helps raise capital resources. (After all, would you lend money to someone who has no plan for using it, or would you rather buy into a well-thought-out program for building profits?)

A plan is a look at where you are and where you hope to go. And then a review of what steps you need to get there.

Usually those steps are in rough chronological order. Some managers look at the plan as their business blueprint. Others call it the management mix, roadmap, game plan, or the directions on the boxtop.

But why do you need these guidelines? Because without sailing orders, the firm is a ship without a rudder, drifting around without a port. Not exactly the image or model of efficiency. And not a good investment.

Also you need a plan simply because no one can remember hundreds of details while busy trying to get dozens of things done. You could waste motion or make major mistakes. Even the best surgeons, pilots and managers work from checklists. To make things easy on yourself, you can think of the wise moves well ahead of time, during your calm planning period. List them. Plot, plan, and scheme. Get your good ideas from other sources, printed material, competition, noncompetitors, trade associations, the market, friends, or almost anywhere. Nobody's smarter than everybody.

Remember: You are competing. Your competitors also have plans. (At least the smart ones do.) You can hope that they don't have this book, so they won't make plans as strong as you will. But, the very fact that your crafty, more aggressive competitors are plotting and planning (with some plans aimed at you), is all the more reason why you should beat them at their own game—before they do the same to you.

You wouldn't build a garage, prepare for a ballgame, make a garment, take a trip, cook a meal, or stage a wedding without a plan. Yet building a business is usually far more expensive and profitable than any of these—and creates greater disaster if it fails—so you certainly want to do at least as much planning. (And maybe a bit more, just to be on the safe side.)

Further, the idea of a self-fulfilling prophesy may not be a sure thing, of course, but there is something to it. Prayers and dreams have come true, partly because the person had a specific goal and dedicated real resources toward achieving it. As Peter Drucker says, "Some people hope. Other people plan." Says the Small Business Association, "Failing to plan is planning to fail."

"OK," you might say, "can you give me a simple plan example?"

Sure. One of the best and easiest kinds of plans just asks four questions: Where are we now? What are our weapons or resources? Where do we want to go? How are we going to get there?

S: *Situation:* Where are we now?

W: *Weapon resources:* What tools do we have?

O: *Objectives:* Where do we want to go?

T: *Tactics/strategy:* How are we going to get there?

In a word, SWOT.

SWOT works particularly well, because it is easy to understand. It's practical and uses common sense. Without even thinking about it, we SWOT our problems every day. We know where we are and what our goals, resources, and tactics are. SWOT is also easy to explain to others. They tend to accept it and like it.

This formula has been used by the ancients in military strategy long before Christ, and today is used by modern armies. It was also used by both prehistoric and modern governments. Today the best managed companies in the world, such as Proctor & Gamble, Merk, Kraft, IBM, 3M, Sony, Rubbermaid, Datson, Suzuki, Liz Claiborne, and Disney (to name but a few) use this sort of planning. And they get excellent results.

If you get nothing more out of this book, then at least remember SWOT. And you will have acquired a tool that can serve you the rest of your life.

For the situation part, you can use the 5 W's; *who* plans and takes action, *what* are the strengths, weaknesses, opportunities, and threats, *when* is the best time to move, *where* is the market, and *why* is the plan made?

In the weapons section, consider your resources and product or service superiorities or skills.

For objectives, think short term, like this year, and long term, for several years.

For tactics, there are usually seven plans: a marketing plan, production plan, finance plan, people plan, outsider plan, selling plan, and time plan. A manager told me that one of his people made up a corny little story to make these seven easy to remember. A man from Finland gave his friend Mark an old post, suggesting he use it for firewood. It didn't burn very well so his wife said, "Mark, prod the Fin POST."

Mark = Marketing Plan

Prod = Production Plan

Fin = Finance Plan

    P = People Plan

    O = Outsider Plan

    S = Selling Plan

    T = Time Plan

Now let's put all this together into a plan outline.

SITUATION

Who	Strengths
What	Weaknesses
When	Opportunities
Where	Threats
Why	

WEAPONS

Resources	Superiorities

OBJECTIVES

Sales	Short term
Profits	Long term

TACTICS

Market Plan	People Plan
Product Plan	Outsider Plan
Finance Plan	Selling the Plan
	Time Plan

And you've got it! Put in some words for each item and you've made a plan. It may not be fancy but it could surpass your competition. Now you know how to do it. And you can put it together almost any time, just by using SWOT.

This gives you three advantages.

First   You have a program. You have a practical, understandable formula. And *you* have it, not someone else. It's yours. It makes you the initiator and the leader.

Second   You provide a major service to your group because you
help them to define things and to clarify any fuzzy
thinking. Anyone can understand SWOT. But most
people want to start with tactics. That jumps the gun
and can hurt the company because it ignores the important elements of situation, resources and objectives.

"Oh, everyone knows all that stuff!" some will say.
But do they really? And do they all agree? Surveys
show that among ten people, only three will agree on
the real problems or goal. Yet nine out of ten will agree
that "a problem well defined is half solved." Defining
problems puts you in the driver's seat.

Third   You bring everyone's thinking together into a common, practical program. You used good ideas from
each person. You generated both unity and personal
involvement. You have agreement on situation, resources, and goals. You may even have an emotional commitment. Now, you will have far less indecision and
debate on your tactical steps. You have given your
group a system they can use and even sell to others.
Psychologically, the planners all feel more comfortable.

In summary, we saw that a plan is simply a program to manage
resources so we produce a profit. It shows where we are, where we
want to go, and how to get there. It builds efficiency, avoids mistakes,
and helps us compete. We looked at the handy SWOT formula: Situation, Weapons, Objectives, and Tactics. The Situation is the 5 W's.
Weapons are simply our resources and superiorities of product and
skills. Objectives are sales and profits, now and later. Tactics come
from the formula, "Mark prod the fin POST" or plans for marketing,
production, finance, people, outsiders, selling the plan, and timing.
You can now lead with a formula, clearly defining things, and gaining group unity on the best steps to take next.

Already, you know more about a strategic plan's contents than
ninety percent of your competitors. Now it's time to learn about the
next steps.

3

How to Write an Effective Title Page

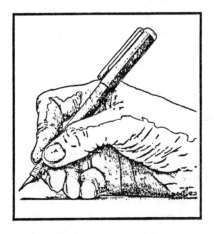

Don't write me a great movie; get me a great title.

— Sam Goldwin

Here we will give you some general guidelines for a title page and then go right to a demonstration. We'll also look at a blank practical project form that you can use to do your own title.

The title page is highly important. Its basic purpose is to identify the document. But it can and should do a whole lot more for you. It sets the stage and establishes a tone for your plan. Initially, of course, it gives your readers the key information they want. But the title page also begins to sell them. There are a dozen subtle devices often used to make it easy for your reader to understand, to keep the plan attractive and interesting, and to get your proposal to stand out above the rest. Remember, your reader may look at a dozen plans that day.

GENERAL GUIDELINES FOR THE TITLE PAGE

1. *Items to include.* Give the name of the plan, company name, address, key manager of the company, his/her phone number, the basic idea of the plan in about twenty-five words or less, the name of the person who prepared the plan, the group to whom the plan is addressed, and the date. You just eliminated a lot of questions, confusion, problems, and perhaps even challenges.

   The twenty-five word basic idea is unusual but especially useful in making your plan stand out, since readers often have difficulty figuring out just what the proposal is about. But they nearly always read the title page, and anything that helps them, helps you. The summary also lets you sell a little.

2. *Type and layout.* The title page becomes more attractive and professional-looking if the title material is either typeset, or has various type sizes, with the title and company most prominent. The material should be nicely spaced down the page, just as most book title pages are laid out. Don't cram it all together at the top. A pleasant layout makes reading easier and pleases the eye.

3. *Artwork.* A photo, sketch, design, or other artwork can be used with excellent results if it is appropriate, in good taste, and not distracting or overwhelming. The covers of annual reports for prominent companies can give you good ideas. (Ask any investment broker for copies.) You can't judge a book by its cover, but covers have sold a lot of books, and a cherry on top has sold a lot of sundaes. The company logo or trademark is often a good option for cover art. It visually identifies the company, gives a businesslike tone and does some selling.

4. *Binder.* A folded, flat, good-quality paper cover is usually a bit better than a three-ring binder, because it is physically easier to route around the office, send in the mail, carry in a briefcase, or put in a file. Remember, the first reader often needs to consult with, sell, and send things to other people. Make the binder convenient, easy, and attractive.

5. The whole, over all impression should be one of professionalism, confidence, reliability. To the reader, it should say, loud and clear, "Here is a company that knows what it is doing—and probably is well worth my investment."

A GOOD TITLE PAGE

A STRATEGIC BUSINESS PLAN FOR EXPANDING CONSULTING SERVICES

Prepared Sept. 3, 1990, for

ABLE, BAKER AND CHARLIE, CPA's

44444 Lexington Ave, New York, NY 10020 Allan B. Able, Managing Partner

Phone — 212/555-8110

Basic idea: Major accounting firms in the market have successfully expanded into management consulting; this plan is a program for doing this in Albany, New York.

Prepared by

American Institute of Management, 1016 Meadow Road, Omaha, NE 68154

Richard D. White, vice-president

402/333-5030

BLANK TITLE PAGE FORM

Title_____

Date prepared _____

Prepared for_____

Address _____

President _____

Phone_____

Basic idea: _____

_____

_____

_____

Prepared by_____

Address _____

Officer _____

Phone _____

4

Making an Executive Summary That Convinces

*Avoid paralysis by analysis. Be prag-
matic, not dogmatic.*
— Peters & Waterman

What is an executive summary? It is a very short condensation of the
entire plan. It is the tip of the iceberg. Generally, much fact gathering
and thought goes on well before the summary is made. Who makes
it? Usually the planner, although almost any sharp business analyst-
writer can make a good summary from a well-prepared complete
plan. When is the summary prepared? In most cases it is easiest to do
after the full plan is prepared, but before it is presented to your key
audience. Where does it appear? Usually right up front, after the title
page. Why is it made? The most typical purposes, objectives or
reasons are to quickly inform and to sell the plan, and to address key
people, such as management, employees, or prospective investors.

An executive summary is very much a sales tool aimed at that top group.

GENERAL GUIDELINES FOR
THE EXECUTIVE SUMMARY

1. Be brief. Most readers, especially major financiers, will spend only about five or ten minutes with a strategic plan. They often read just the title page and the executive summary. Together those should total about three to six pages, so just hit the highlights.

2. Be especially well prepared, and polished. Accurately condense the longer plan. Summaries are usually the best-read part of almost any document, including a plan document.

3. Keep the summary plain, clear, simple, and to the point. Weigh every word. Make every one count. Each costs something and gains something; make sure of a net gain. Sentence fragments are OK, if the meaning is clear. Rather than making dramatic claims or promises, provide dramatic facts. Let these speak for themselves and have their own impact.

4. Be well tuned. Decide whom you are addressing. Identify their key interests. Speak to those interests.

5. Briefly cover the SWOT points (situation), especially the opportunities and trends in the market; the Resources (weapons) of the company, especially product advantages and a simple balance sheet; the Objectives for sales and profits; and then the Tactical plans for reaching those goals.

6. If your audience is financial people, they immediately will look for at least a brief cash flow projection, return on investment (ROI) and a key cost/expense item schedule. Indicate funds needed and when these are to generate profits and be repaid.

7. Link it all together. Show how each part fits. Where supporting details are clearly needed, promptly refer the reader to

the larger document. Be very up-front, open, and factual. Take extra effort to show that you are not hiding any key fact. Give every appearance of candor. This is important in building reader confidence. Some things must be taken on trust. Investors are usually suspicious of everything, and with good reason. They've been burned. Make them trust you.

The following demonstration is a little more detailed than is usually needed. It shows how to include key points under every one of the subjects. In reality, you might skip or minimize some of these subjects.

EXECUTIVE SUMMARY — Able, Baker and Charlie, CPA's, Inc.

Our format here follows the formula professional planners (P & G, and others) often use to cover their investment strategies: SWOT—Situation, Weapon resources, Objectives, and Tactics. This has made our past planning easier and more profitable.

1. Our situation

Some of the nation's top CPA firms, our competitors, have been opening management consulting departments. Because surveys show that accountants are among the most trusted business colleagues, these new consultant activities have prospered. Some, in a few years, far surpass the profits of the long-established CPA practices. Our plan is to do the same thing, but do it better — with a far more careful plan and qualified people. We believe that it can show a 40% ROI after the second year.

Market opportunities (feasibility). A survey of our current twenty Albany accounting clients shows that 95% like the consulting idea. Half said they know of more prospects. Five have even helped design this plan. Three are ready to sign up now. Each of these three spends $100,000 a year for specialized management consulting services. Most clients indicated we could fill this need. Consultant services currently are a bit short, especially in our area of service accounting and service consulting (although this could change).

2. Weapon resources

Our strengths are threefold: We know the market and have clients ready to sign. The general CPA market is successfully moving in this direction. We have several high-quality, proven professional people available at favorable cost. Also, we have the capital to provide about a third of the program.

Balance sheet in summary (thousands):

Current assets (cash, etc.)	$50	Cur. liabil.	$20
Fixed asts. (bldg., equip.)	60	Long-term liabil.	50
Other asts. (intang.)	10	Net worth	50
Total	$120	Total	$120

Total package investment for Albany is $100,000, first year. Details are in document.

Costs/expense schedule (thousands):

Staff $60

Equipment (used) 10

Rent/utilities 6

Travel/advertising 10

Supplies, tax, other 14

Total $100

The Albany program would need $100,000. ABC-CPAs can put in $35,000 as an equity injection from the cash assets shown above. $65,000 is needed as a ten-year loan.

Our weaknesses are that this is a fairly new field to us. Our opportunities are the current trends and unfilled demand. Our threats are the uncertain actions of competitors.

3. Objectives

Profit and Loss Projection (thousands):

	1stQ	2ndQ	3rdQ	4thQ	5thQ	6thQ
Billing forecast	$50	$100	$250	$400	$450	$500
Cost to operate	25	50	125	200	225	270
Other costs(*)	75	100	125	150	150	170
Profit (loss)	(50)	(50)	0	50	75	60
Cumulative	(50)	(100)	(100)	(50)	25	85

(*) Includes loan repayment @ $6 per qtr.

4. Market Plan (tactics)

Prospects. A number of our clients are good prospects and will recommend us to others. The Albany Chamber of Commerce lists 10,000 metro firms (within 50 miles). 30% (3,000) are service firms. 500 hire consultants. Some have serious problems. We have these lists.

Advertising. We have a collection of tested and proven (competitive) direct mail brochures. Plus our ad agency has four new, tested concepts. Monthly blitz to the 500 who do the hiring. Some one-fourth page print are ads planned for the chamber magazine.

Public appearances, weekly, by local director can be arranged with chamber and other business groups.

Personal follow-up phone calls are planned for the top 50 companies each month. We will seek permission to put on a 30-minute presentation.

Personal presentations feature slides and flip charts of our service benefits, the common consultant mistakes clients should avoid, and how to get the most from a consultant. We will close with a summary booklet, some testimonial reference letters, case histories of our client successes over the past year, sample short-form business plans, and our book on business planning, as well as resumes of our top people and a contract.

Sales forecast. We expect a 1% return on the top 500 (or 5 new clients per month, 60 a year). The average billing: $10,000 (or $600,000 annually). We expect $800,000 the first year (see P & L above).

Our price: $600/day. (Night work and research, no charge).

Our product: a professional report (with special presentation).

5. Production plan

Consulting schedules should have no problem meshing in with the sales volume forecast and sales/marketing. Production based on known management consultant patterns anticipates one project per consultant per week (or fifty per consultant per year). Three consultants means 150 projects a year. The first year we expect 50% of this rate weekly (or one project every two weeks). Seventy-five for the year.

6. Finance plan

Finance plan (thousands):

	Year 1	Year 2
Est. billing	$800	$1,100
Est. costs	750	970
Profit/loss	($50)	$130

This yields a cumulative profit figure of $80,000, which translates to an annual 40% ROI. (For loan needs and cost schedule, see items 2 and 3 above.) We anticipate repaying the $100,000 loan after the third year.

7. Our people plan is unusually favorable

We have intermittently provided CPA service for three major service companies in the area, three of whose special senior officers took early retirement one or two years ago. Since then, these three have been serving as volunteer service management consultants to smaller or mid-sized firms, and have won major local business community awards and press recognition. All three of these have indicated a strong desire to join ABC in this venture on a very modest salary, serving only part time as needed. They remain as major stockholders to their past firms (currently not our clients) and they have deep contacts with most key firms in the area.

8. Outsider plan

ABC has long-standing, close associations with a major Albany bank, a law firm, the chamber of commerce, the local print and broadcast media, an ad agency, trade associations, and service clubs. Many of these indicate they will recommend us to prospective clients.

9. Short sales presentation of entire strategic plan

A short sales presentation of this entire strategic plan was designed by our ad agency and is available for any person or group. This includes color slides and flip charts on the market, financial projections, (P&L, cash flow, expense schedule, loan and repayment schedule), plans for marketing, the organization, resumes on all personnel, client prospect lists, client contract forms, and copies of this executive summary.

10. Time plan, the next three steps

Person(s)	Action	Planned Date
Loan committee	Approve loan, set up accounts.	Nov. 1, l990
ABC Manager	Final lease on space, equip. obtain staff, start advertising	Dec. 3, 1990
Albany manager	Open h'se recept'n sign clients	Jan 11, 1991

We sincerely hope you can participate in this sound plan.

Respectfully submitted,
Allan D. Able, Mging Partner   Richard D White, Vice-President
Able, Baker and Charlie, CPA's   American Inst. of Mgmt.

EXECUTIVE SUMMARY FORM

Title _____

Format or introduction statement_____

_____

1. SITUATION, Market Opportunities (Feasibility)

Prospects opinions _____

_____

Who will buy and why_____

_____

Product advantages _____

Remarks _____

2. WEAPON RESOURCES

Staff skills _____

Capital available _____

Investment needed_____

Remarks _____

3. OBJECTIVES

P&L Forecast	Per.1	Per.2	Per.3	Per.4
Sales	____	____	____	____
All costs	____	____	____	____
Profit/loss	____	____	____	____

Remarks _____

4. MARKET PLAN

Product _____ Package _____

Price_____ Premium _____

Physical Distribution _____ Publicity _____

Advertising theme _____

Ad media (key) _____

Remarks _____

5. PRODUCTION PLAN (Output per month)

Product	Jan	Feb	Mar	Apr	May	Jun	Jul	Aug	Sept	Oct	Nov	Dec
A	___	___	___	___	___	___	___	___	___	___	___	___
B	___	___	___	___	___	___	___	___	___	___	___	___

Remarks _____

6. FINANCE PLAN

Capital investment _____

Profits lst year _____ 2nd Year _____ 3rd year _____

Time (qtr) break even _____ ROI the next qtr _____

Remarks _____

7. PEOPLE PLAN

Specs _____

Job Description _____

Recruiting steps _____

Training _____

Wage and benefits _____

Remarks _____

8. OUTSIDER PLAN

Accountant _____ Lawyer _____

Banker _____ Supplier _____

Adv. Agency _____ Local Chamber of Commerce _____

Mgmt. Consult. _____ Trade Assns _____

Remarks _____

9. SELLING THE PLAN (Material available)

Flips/slides_____ Product. Steps _____

Facts _____ Organiz. Chart_____

Goals _____ Time Sched. _____

Mkt. steps _____ Plan handout_____

Remarks _____

10. TIME PLAN, NEXT THREE STEPS

	Who	Does what	When
1.	_____	_____	_____
2.	_____	_____	_____
3.	_____	_____	_____

Remarks _____

Submitted by:

_____   _____

_____   _____

5

Situation:

How to Gather Market Facts

To succeed, do those things known to cause success.

— P & G Slogan

The first letter of SWOT, the stands for the situation or conditions facing us in the market. This means we should take a close look at our market strengths, weaknesses, opportunities, and threats. First, we should look outwards, toward our market and our industry.

Consider the positive power of facts.

- Most failed projects occur through mistakes (read: ignorance).

- Most successful people credit wisdom.

- Most failures occur because managers are too impatient to gather necessary information.

- Major mistakes and bad guesses can ruin firms and careers.

- Management is right only about 50 percent of the time.

- Four out of five new ventures fail. (That's 80 percent!)

- Many managers prefer to guess—to prove they're macho.

- Facts protect investment and people's jobs.

- In poker, business, war, and games, knowledge is really power.

- The cost getting facts is much less than costs of failure.

- The modern manager's biggest mistake is miserable communication.

- Most mistakes can be prevented by reviewing low-cost facts.

Information expensive? Try ignorance!

"OK, facts are vital. But how do I get them?" you might say. Let's look at your 4 W's for fact gathering:

Who: Probably you with a close helper, if possible.

What: A set of basic facts outlined next.

When: Quick as you can. Time is money.

Why: To cut chance of failure. Build chance of success.

Begin by making it easy; convince yourself of the value. Recognize that every added fact you find can help save you many days and hundreds of dollars (perhaps avoiding a major, disastrous error) and build your success. Each fact is a piece of the jigsaw puzzle. With this in mind, you will find fact gathering to be interesting, rewarding, and even fun.

Caution. Investing too much time, money, and resources to get more facts than are needed is a poor return on investment. Some companies spend years gathering too many facts. This is often a thinly disguised method for avoiding a decision. Some books on planning are really 95% analysis. The result is that we drown in data and starve for knowledge.

Use your own best judgment. A serious problem or project deserves more research than a minor one. Gather as much as you can easily afford within a reasonable timeframe. Learn enough so that you feel comfortable that you know what you are doing. Get enough to answer basic questions about your industry, market, and company. Your colleagues, boss, and bankers will want to know that you know. A day or week is usually too little time. A year may be too much. A few weeks is usually about right.

In the next few pages, you will find an explanation, a demonstration, and a practical project form for you to use.

EXPLANATION

Your easiest beginning is the 5 W's. This gives you a fast, short, manageable structure and guides you to a more complete analysis; Who, What, When, Where, Why . . . all directed *outside* the company, towards your market and your industry.

"Who" should first cover your customers. Who they are. Who is buying now. Who will buy in the future. Give a description of your best prospects, then your second and third best. Isolate demographic factors: location, age, income, sex, occupation, trends, opinions, wants, needs, likes and dislikes, gripes and preferences.

The "who" also means who are your competitors. Who are "the brands to beat"? How good are they? What are their strengths, weaknesses, opportunities, tactics?

"What" means what are you selling. If you are selling a product, are your customers really buying the service that product brings? (Drucker says, "All products are services.") What service? What are your superiorities—in what way is it better than competition? What can your competition's products, advertising and promotion tell or teach you? What prospect wants and needs does your product/service fill? What are the benefits to your customers? What can be done to improve your product or service? Should this be done? What do your customers say about your product—good and bad?

What is the market? The size, in dollars and units, by outlet and by year? Trends? Is it growing, dying, static, changing? What are some attractive market segment opportunities? What causes industry market growth and decline? Is seasonality a factor? The market leaders: what part of the industry cycle are they in; start, growth, mature, decline? What is your share of the total market? What is the trend of your sales, your profit and your share? What does it take to get a bigger share. What are the key factors to success (Quality, package, price, promotion, physical distribution, reputation?)

When do customers buy? When are the best months? The worst? When should you plan next year's programs, products and production?

Where do customers make their purchases? What are the distribution channels? Where are the best places to sell, and where are the worst?

Why do your customers buy from you? Why from your competitors?

The 8 P's of market planning are a useful formula to guide industry fact gathering. This is especially helpful in the first page or two of a marketing "strategy" plan. In that sense, gathering such data does double duty, by providing key information in this section to generally assist other sections, and becoming the actual first part of the strategic market plan covered in a specific later section.

The 8 P's often used by major marketing strategists are; Product, Package, Price, Premiums, Promotions, Physical distribution, Personal selling and Publicity/advertising. A chart showing these items for top brands in the market can be a useful tool. It can show where you may be strong and where you need to do some work.

"Where do I find all that information?"

Your best sources are either within your company, or outside sources that are often nearby and may cost nothing.

The inside sources include

1. Your marketing, sales, advertising, market research, or public relations people. They can usually fill in at least half of the data required.

2. Other inside people, including supervisors, colleagues, and other employees.

Outside sources include

1. Trade associations and journals (they prepare market and industry surveys and data, often in great detail, free for the asking).

2. The SBA, which has three major groups, each with large amounts of free information. First, SCORE or the

Service Corps of Retired Executives. Second, SBI or the Small Business Institute: graduate students who do surveys and research usually worth over $6,000—at no cost to you. Third is the SBDC or Small Business Development Centers. Located at most major American universities, SBDCs use professors, graduate students, and advanced electronic equipment to provide large amounts of information free or at low cost.

3. The local library, which often has considerable published information on markets and industries.

4. The U.S. Department of Commerce.

5. Local management consultants.

6. Outside research organizations, such as A.C. Nielsen.

Other sources include local friends and business associates or suppliers, such as your advertising agency.

DEMONSTRATION

Here's an example of how all this comes together in an actual market/industry review. Some parts are blank, because in the real world, very few small firms can gather all the data called for. In these places we will say, "Coming later, as opportunities permit." The company below is a small service firm—an advertising agency—that also publishes college manuals. It is fictional, but based on several similar firms.

Company: <u>American Innovation Makers</u>

Address: <u>20608 Greenwood Drive, Olympia Fields, IL 12345</u>

Who are our present customers? <u>Small consumer goods manufacturers who advertise</u>

Who are our potential customers? <u>More of this same type of firm</u>

Who are our best prospects? <u>Same type, with product superiorities in large dollar markets. More data coming later</u>

Second best? Same type, few superiorities, small markets

Third best? Same type, no superiorities, small markets

Prospect location: Metro Chicago area. Age: Any. Income: $1 to $5 million in sales

Customer trends: Metro area has shown an 8% increase per year for the last three years for this type of business

Prospects Opinions: Survey shows most prospects want and need sales messages that are both creative and effective

Likes and preferences: Unusually well-prepared, well-designed, and effective marketing plans

Gripes and dislikes: Poor, superficial, ill-prepared, shallow, wasteful programs

Who are our competitors? Many small, local ad agencies serving consumer package goods manufacturers

The competitor to beat: Gold & Steel, Michigan Avenue

How good are they: Very good: up 20% a year for the last 5 years

Their strengths: Very high creativity

Their weakness: Top management turnover, lack of agency marketing

Their opportunities: To build on reputation & success of clients

Their tactics: High focus on filling client needs

Their product: Good advertising, gets high ROI for marketing

Their price: 15% commission plus fees on some services

Their package: Good facilities, sign, logo, brochure

Their promotions: Very few; no marketing program for agency

Their physical distribution: Limited to metro Chicago

Their personal selling: Mainly account exec. service + clients

Their PR & Advertising: None; let performance sell agency

What are we selling? <u>Good service, good relations, good results</u>

What are our superiorities? <u>Research and agency marketing</u>

What do competitors teach us? <u>Market self as well as client</u>

What customers want do we provide? <u>Good ads & marketing</u>

What customer benefits do we provide? <u>Sales results. ROI</u>

What can we do to improve? <u>More prospect opinions</u>

What do prospect say? <u>"Never heard of Amer. Innovat. Makers."</u>

What is the total $ market? <u>About $100 mil. this type client</u>

What trends? <u>Up 8% a year</u> Our potential: <u>$5 million/yr</u>

What are good market segment opportunities? <u>Food and beverage ads.</u>

What causes growth of ad volume? <u>Good results of past ads</u>

What seasonality? <u>Major program planned in Sept.-Nov</u>

What share do we have? <u>1%</u> Our sales trend: <u>Up 5% a year</u>

What is needed to build share? <u>Aggressive marketing of agency</u>

What are keys to success? <u>Learn customer needs, fill these</u>

When do customers buy? <u>Most change agencies in June-Sept.</u>

When plan client programs? <u>Sept.-Nov. Research: June-Sept.</u>

When produce product (advertising):? <u>Oct.-Nov.</u>

Where do customers buy? <u>Personal contact; phone; mail</u>

Where are best places to sell? <u>Start with mail, then phone</u>

Where is best geographic area? <u>Locally. But reach. U.S., Europe</u>

Why do customers buy? <u>Convenience; awareness; confidence;</u>
<u>good human relations; good sales results</u>

OUR 8 Ps (market facts)

Our Product: <u>Effective advertising</u>

Our Price: <u>15% Commission + fee schedule on services</u>

Our Package: <u>Our signs, logo, slogan, location, brochure</u>

Our Promotion: <u>Has been mainly occasional luncheon talks</u>

Our Premiums: <u>Free advice on conference forms; data mailings</u>

Our Physical distribution: <u>We currently serve metro Chicago</u>

Our Personal selling: <u>Lunch talks, conference panels</u>

Our PR and adv.: <u>Short items to media and mail pieces</u>

MARKET FACTS FORM

Company: _____

Address: _____

Who are our present customers?_____

Who are potential customers? _____

Who are best prospects? _____

Second best? _____

Third best? _____

Prospect location: _____

Prospect trends: _____

Prospect opinions: _____

Likes and preferences:_____

Gripes and dislikes: _____

Who are our competitors? _____

Who's the competitor to beat?_____

How good are they? _____

Their strengths:_____

Their weaknesses: _____

Their opportunities:_____

Their tactics: _____

Their product: _____

Their price: _____

Their package: _____

Their promotions: _____

Their physical distribution: _____

Their personal selling:_____

Their PR & advertising:_____

What are we selling? _____

What are our superiorities? _____

What do our competitors teach us?_____

What customer wants do we provide?_____

What customer benefits do we provide? _____

What can we do to improve? _____

What do prospects say about us? _____

What is the total $ market?_____

What trends?_____ What's our potential?_____

What are good market segment opportunities?_____

What causes industry growth?_____

What seasonality?_____

What share do we have? _____ Our sales trend:_____

What is needed to build share? _____

What are keys to success? _____

When do customers buy?_____

When plan client programs?_____

When produce product (timeline)?_____

Where do customers buy? _____

Where are best places to sell?_____

Where is best geographic area? _____

Why do customers buy?_____

OUR 8 Ps (market facts)

Our Product: _____

Our Price: _____

Our Package: _____

Our Promotions: _____

Our Premiums: _____

Our Physical distribution: _____

Our Personal selling: _____

Our PR and adv:_____

Fill out this form as best you can. Then let others in your group help you. That should cover 80 percent. Then get outside help. Some data may not be worth the cost of tracking down, but some may be well worth it.

When finished, or nearly so, you will know more about the market and the industry than most anyone in your firm—and probably more than most of your competitors. You will know where the dangers are and where the opportunities lie. You are in a great position to do some aggressive and efficient planning.

6

Weapon Resources:

How to Gather Useful Company Facts

You will never have all the facts and you don't need them. Just get enough.
— Henry Adams

We just finished looking at the S or Situation part of the SWOT formula. Now we will review our W or Weapon resources. Essentially, that means we look at our company.

BENEFITS

In checking our market and industry facts, we reviewed some reasons to gather data. These reasons can be recapped with the following checklist. It begins when we ask ourselves, "Which of these benefits would I like from market facts?" (While they all apply, just check the ones you like.)

( ) 1. to avoid sales drops   ( ) 7. to out-do your competitors
( ) 2. to gain insight   ( ) 8. to protect your company
( ) 3. to go at proper speed   ( ) 9. to protect employee jobs
( ) 4. to cut normal costs   ( )10. to get Knowledge Power
( ) 5. to improve judgment   ( )11. to avoid costly disasters
( ) 6. to avoid serious error   ( )12. to improve data flow

The bottom line on benefits: Facts help you work smarter (not harder), give you more bang for your buck, and help you generate more effective plans without spinning your wheels. The Japanese are vigorous fact gatherers and planners. They plan their work and work their plan. And they make excellent progress. Their productivity is often seven times ours, yet they learned much of this marketing strategy from America!

How can you gather facts quickly and at low cost?

1. Start with a simple checklist, such as you have here.

2. Ask immediate managers, associates, and colleagues.

3. Check other sources, such as accountants, lawyers, auditors, ad agencies, libraries, trade associations, and others.

Fill in the blanks as best you can. Don't get hung up on any one item. If you don't have the data, make an estimate or skip it. At least you will know where the holes are.

What kind of data should you collect about your company? Certainly you want to have a brief history: key managers; employees; advisors; what you sell; when, where, and how you sell it; and your financial picture. And be sure to include your situation, strengths, weaknesses, resources, trends and causes, plus possibilities for takeover, buyout, sellout, startup, or expansion.

For your company analysis we will explain, demonstrate, and then provide a form for you to use.

EXPLANATION

You should begin by looking at a brief history of the company: how and when it started, how it grew, and what it's like today.

The familiar 5 W's are a useful way to get a quick fix.

Who means "people." Who started the business, who manages it, and who it serves. Who are your employees or key groups? What are their skills, knowledge, abilities, your experience, and roles? Who are your key advisors: your accountant, lawyer, banker, board members, advertising agency, suppliers, collection agency?

What means "things." What is the nature of your company? What is your real business? What does the company sell? What service does it perform? What is the legal form of the business (proprietorship, partnership, corporation)?

When means "time." When do you sell the most and the least? When do you see the most profits? When do business cycles effect you most and least?

Where means "location." Where is the ideal place to put your business? Where is the worst location?

Why means "reason, purpose or goal." Why was the company started? Why did it grow? Why do people now buy from the company?

In addition, a financial analysis is important because it can tell you how weak or strong you are, how sick or healthy. It does this in a page or two. It should cover by year sales, costs, net before taxes, taxes, net after tax. If the profit trend is going down, you have a problem. It should also show (by years) assets and liabilities and equity. If your liabilities exceed your assets, you have a serious problem.

Is the business involved in a buy out or takeover, a start-up, or expansion? If you are involved in a takeover: When? By whom? Why is the seller selling and the buyer buying? At what price? How much "blue sky." Is it fair? Why? What are the sales and profit trends of the seller? Are they declining? Can the buyer change this?

If you are involved in a start-up: When? By whom? Why will it succeed? Who are the advisors, suppliers, and key managers?

An expansion plan is probably most likely. Therefore, the material in this book applies especially to business building. However, as such, these programs clearly apply to start-ups and takeovers.

The strengths of your company will have been well analyzed, if you covered the 5 W's, and particularly if you listed special skills and talents in the who section and product or service superiorities in the what section.

The weaknesses might be listed in a separate paragraph. This is sometimes a touchy subject: managers don't often want to admit to weaknesses, nor do stockholders wish to focus on these. Therefore these flaws might be stated carefully, not negatively, but in terms of areas that can be improved. Therefore, you can turn a weakness into an opportunity. For example, "We have excellent A-type products and services, yet we have a low awareness and image for these products among some of our key market areas."

The opportunities, in relation to company analysis, are often new, high potential products or services or suppliers. Other opportunities might include sharp growth in sales or profits for your products or services, or a list of skills, knowledge, abilities, technology, concepts, ideas, systems, and programs that have not been fully recognized, developed or applied. Example: "We have talented people in field B and plan to move into that market soon."

Threats within the company include aging, illness, or loss of key personnel or services, suppliers, or advisors; inability to maintain up-to-date training, product, or service problems or liabilities; threatening or dangerous litigation; poor or nonexistent planning or fact gathering; or conflicts between managers, board members, bankers, shareholders. Also, negative internal trends such as rising or excessive costs, declining sales or profits, or excessive debt liabilities would all fall into this category.

Company resources should be recognized and highlighted. These might include special people, facilities and equipment, technologies, research, testing, space, inventories, storage, material handling, and outside contacts listed by size and location. These might also indicate internal trends (such as technical growth or decline) and reasons for this. Also important is the level of corporate integration both backward and forward. Examples: the company may own some of its own material suppliers (backward) or its own channels of distribution or even some of its own customers (forward).

DEMONSTRATION

How does this look when applied to an actual business? Consider this case: a small food manufacturer (a bottler of soft drinks) employing about 30 people. It is fictional, but based on fact.

Company name: Frosty Fizz Bottling, Inc.

Location: 1215 Sunrise Ave., Denver, CO., 13474

Brief History: Frosty Fizz was founded by Jim Walters in December 1946. Jim began the business by installing some used bottling equipment in an old warehouse, and introducing a line of quality, flavored soft drinks to the southeast quarter of Denver. The products were well accepted, partly because the only other bottler supplying that area was a cola firm and people wanted flavors. Since then, Frosty Fizz has grown steadily, and was well entrenched when, in recent years, the cola bottlers introduced their own flavor lines. Frosty Fizz is still a strong brand in the market.

Who manages: Jim Walters sold out in 1975 to Steve Scott, who is the current president. Key managers are Al Able, production supervisor, Bill Baker the marketing director, and Carol Chase the office manager. Dave Dart manages the ten truck drivers (route men) and their equipment.

Employees: 10 route men, 5 helpers, 10 production people, 2 office clerks, 2 maintenance people, 4 managers.

Skills: Each employee was selected because of strong knowledge, abilities and performance in their field. Careful comparison selection plus strong motivation by management has helped to generate unusually high spirits and enthusiasm.

Key advisors:

Accountant: Mr. A.

Lawyer: Ms. B.

Banker: Mr. C.

Board Members: Messrs. D,E,F, & G; Ms. H; and Ms. I.

Suppliers: J Company for flavors, packaging. K for others.

Ad Agency: L and Assoc.

Collection agency: None.

What the business is: To make and sell quality soft drinks.

What the purpose is: To provide profits, a good return on in- vestment, good service to our customers, and good jobs.

What we sell: A quality line of flavored soft drinks.

What the legal form of the business is: A corporation.

When we sell: 70% is sold in the 6 months Apr-Sep.

Why we grew: Strict adherence to quality, plus good marketing: prices, promotions, displays, availability.

Why people buy now: Same reasons.

FINANCIAL ANALYSIS:

Profit & Loss Statements, Last 4 Years, Condensed (thousands)

ITEM	Year 1	Year 2	Year 3	This Year, 4
Sales	$2,000	$3,500	$4,000	$5,000
Cost goods	1,000	1,750	2,000	2,500
Gross profits	$1,000	$1,750	$2,000	$2,500
Administration	300	350	400	450
Selling	600	700	800	900
Other	600	1,000	300	350
Total costs	$1,500	$2,050	$1,500	$1,700
Net before taxes	($500)	($300)	500	800
Tax	0	0	200	300
Net After Taxes	($500)	($300)	300	500

Trends and causes: Clearly the company was showing sharp losses, but it has made steady improvement. Major cause of the loss was high "other" costs. These included research and development, trying to create a new, low calorie soft drink and confection line. This was accomplished, costs went down, sales and profits went up.

BALANCE SHEET

Last 4 Years, Condensed (thousands)

Item	Year 1	Year 2	Year 3	This Year, 4
Assets				
Current	600	700	800	500
Fixed	700	1,000	1,600	2,000
Total Assets	$1,300	$1,700	$2,400	$2,500
Liabilities				
Debt, short	600	700	800	800
Debt, long	1,000	1,100	1,300	1,100
Equity (net worth)	(300)	(100)	300	600
Total Liability	$1,300	$1,700	$2,400	$2,500

Trends and causes: Clearly the company was in a serious financial situation in years one and two. Debt exceeded assets, putting the firm into negative net worth. But the situation has brightened greatly in the last two years, due in part to the success of the new low-calorie products.

Takeover/buy out: Yes; Frosty Fizz distributorship in Boulder has been a break-even operation, at best, for some years. The manager is buying the operation. The price is $100,000, which is more than fair, considering the assets and the profit picture. Changes are planned that should improve the profits.

Start-up/expansion: Yes; the new low calorie soft drink and confections (candy, cookies, and ice cream) will be franchised.

Strengths: Improving profits, long strong reputation for quality products. Good, skilled, enthusiastic staff. Exciting, potential high profit new products. Good advisors.

Weaknesses: <u>Still low awareness and image of new products. Low</u> <u>capitalization support for major new product introduction.</u>

Opportunities: <u>Good new low-calorie products in high-potential</u> <u>markets.</u>

Threats: <u>Temptation for rapid expansion. Strong competition.</u>

Resources: <u>Good plant, equipment, staff, products, and suppliers.</u>

COMPANY FACTS FORM

Company name: _____

Location: _____

Brief history: _____

Company manager: _____

Employees (groups):_____

Key advisors: _____

What the business is: _____

What the purpose is:_____

What we sell:_____

What our legal form of business is: _____

When we sell (best):_____

Why we grew: _____

PROFIT-AND-LOSS FORM

Last 4 Years (in thousands)

	Year 1	Year 2	Year 3	This Year, 4
Sales	_____	_____	_____	_____
Cost goods	_____	_____	_____	_____
Gross Profits	_____	_____	_____	_____
Administration costs	_____	_____	_____	_____
Sell costs	_____	_____	_____	_____
Other costs	_____	_____	_____	_____
Total costs	_____	_____	_____	_____
Net Before Taxes	_____	_____	_____	_____
Tax	_____	_____	_____	_____
Net After Taxes	_____	_____	_____	_____

Trends and causes: _____

BALANCE SHEET FORM

Last 4 years (in thousands)

	Year 1	Year 2	Year 3	This Year, 4
Assets				
Current	_____	_____	_____	_____
Fixed	_____	_____	_____	_____
Total	_____	_____	_____	_____
Liabilities				
Debt, short	_____	_____	_____	_____
Debt, long	_____	_____	_____	_____
Equity	_____	_____	_____	_____
Total Liability	_____	_____	_____	_____

Trends and causes: _____

_____

Takeover/buy out: _____

Start-up/expansion:_____

Strengths: _____

Weaknesses:_____

Opportunities: _____

Threats: _____

Company resources:_____

Use all or most of this form and you will have a very good grasp of company facts. You will have a good basis for further planning. And you will know a lot more about your company than most competitors know about theirs. You will have a valuable advantage.

7

Objectives And How To Set Them

Columbus didn't just sail, he sailed west.

— Golightly

Our purpose here is to provide you with some good reasons to set goals, emphasizing benefits to you and your company. We'll look at some good, typical goals you might elect to use, then some general guidelines for making them. In all, we'll explain about goals, demonstrate goals, and then provide a practical project form for you to use.

EXPLANATION

Goals or objectives fit in with SWOT since SWOT stands for Situation, Weapon resources, Objectives, and Tactics. We just looked inside at the company and outside at the market and industry. That showed us your Situation and your Weapons or resources. Now it is time to set your goals or objectives.

Don't get confused by words that mean the same as goals. Some planners try to shave things very fine and draw a line between goals and objectives. That is all right, if the differences are clearly spelled out. However to the average manager there is little difference. The easy and practical approach is to recognize that mission, objective, goal, and target all mean essentially the same thing to most people. They mean the place we want to get to or the thing we want to accomplish.

Some people confuse objectives with tactics or strategy. The easy way to avoid that is to always remember that goals means "where" you want to go. Tactics or strategy always mean "how" you plan to get there, your means, system, or methods.

Note: Sometimes an action that might be an objective to one group might be a strategy to another. Example: New staff and new products are a strategy (the means to an end, not an end in itself) to top management. But it is a goal (or end in itself) to personnel and research/development groups.

We usually know where we are (our situation) and we know what our resources are (time, money, energy, etc.). Then we know what we want to accomplish. And finally we decide what methods we will use. We do this many times every day.

Use the handy TO formula. Any time you can say, "I want TO accomplish X" or "I hope TO reach Y" or "I want TO achieve Z," you have a goal. Think of any game; cards, checkers, or baseball. In every case you know what it is you want TO accomplish. That is your objective.

Your benefits. Now that we have a clear insight as to what goals are, let's look at some reasons we should set them, expressed in terms of things that objectives can do for you. Goals give you at least six benefits:

1. Objectives are almost the heart of your whole effort. Goals may be stated only briefly, in a page or even a sentence, but they are your reason for being in business. Few people engage in poker, business, war, or games just for the heck of it. They want to win, or at least to gain some points.

2. Your goals often indicate or point you to your best and smartest tactics or strategies. Big goals need big

programs. You don't stop a tank with a fly swatter; you don't kill a bug with a cannon.

3. Goals let you manage by objective (MBO). This may be a worn-out phrase but it is still worthwhile. MBO means you aim all your efforts at your main purpose. If the action doesn't help reach your goal, then you don't do it. This cuts waste and saves you time, money, and energy.

   MBO helps you avoid disputes. When you all agree on goals, you are far more likely to agree on strategy.

   And MBO gets everyone into the act. It lets people participate. (When people set their own goals, they usually set higher ones then you would ask of them, because they believe in themselves and want to prove something to you.) This unifies the group and generates valuable action and enthusiasm.

Example of a simple goal: "To reach sales of $1 million next year." A more complex goal: "To reach sales of $¼ million each quarter, with 50% from the southeast states, providing profits before taxes of $100K with a 20% ROI."

Make your goals:

1. Both short-range (this year) and long-range (the next few years).

2. Both quantitative and qualitative. (That is, both profits and improved image.)

3. Clear. Put them in writing; give them a specific time frame.

4. Measurable, so they can be compared with actual results. (Have several, so you will hit at least one, but not so many that they become impractical or hard to remember. The more goals, the less focus. Four to eight is a good range.)

5. Challenging

6. Attainable. Avoid the tragedy of excessive expectations. Goals should be realistic, reasonable, reachable,

and beatable. Avoid hidden goals, and don't be over-specific. (Don't say something like, "Increase sales by 12.65% by October 12.")

In addition, be sure to:

1. Allow for some game playing. "The boss wants this goal listed." Lose a battle to win a war if you must.

2. Have a fallback position. "Sales up 12%—or no less than 8%."

3. Be flexible. Drop obsolete goals. Pick up new targets as circumstances change.

4. See that your goals fit both your company's and your top management's mission.

5. Set goals for both routine projects (like sales and production) plus more specialized items (like training programs, strengths to exploit, or weaknesses to solve).

6. State when your goals are based on certain assumptions such as economy, market, or industry trends, and identify these factors.

7. Avoid at all costs setting goals that are totally incompatible with available resources of time, money, staff, and skills.

Recognize the value of incentives. Sometimes you must have stars in your eyes to get off the ground. Many successful projects started out with goals that were never realized.

Ask hard-nosed questions like:

1. How much can we really invest in the first quarter?

2. How much sales volume/profit can we really see each quarter?

3. What do other companies our size say about on these points?

4. Can we stand a loss? How much?

SAMPLE DEMONSTRATION

Strategic Planning Objectives (in thousands)

Goal/Item	1-6 Mo.	2-6 Mo.	1st Yr.	2nd Yr.	Long Term
Market Investment	$1,000	$750	$1,750	$1,500	$1,300/yr
Sales	10,000	15,000	25,000	35,000	45,000
Awareness/image	up	up big	up big	growing	growing
Net profit after taxes	1,000	2,000	3,000	7,000	10,000
Production efficiency	75%	80%	85%	90%	95%
Stock sales (shares)	4	5	9	12	15
Train'g conf.(#)	2	1	3	3	3
New staff (#)	10	10	20	10	10
New products (#)	2	3	5	4	4

COMMENTS

Market investment: This is strategy, of course, not a goal but is included here only to put the other goals in perspective.

Sales: This is net sales, all product lines. This is a key result area!

Awareness/image: Reputation among consumers, others in industry.

Net Profit: After taxes. This is a key result area!

Production efficiency: Refers to plant output versus capacity.

Stock sales: Shares (000's) to be sold by company.

Training conferences: These are actual numbers, not thousands

New staff: Actual numbers. Needed as sales goals are reached.

New products: These are key to reaching sales goals.

Strategic Planning Objectives (in thousands)

Goal/Item	1-6 Mo.	2-6 Mo.	1st Yr.	2nd Yr.	Long Term
Market Investment	$ _____	$ _____	$ _____	$ _____	$ _____
Sales	$ _____	$ _____	$ _____	$ _____	$ _____
Awareness/image					
Net Profit after taxes	$ _____	$ _____	$ _____	$ _____	$ _____
Production Efficiency (%)	_____	_____	_____	_____	_____
Stock sales	_____	_____	_____	_____	_____
Training Conferences#	_____	_____	_____	_____	_____
New staff (#)	_____	_____	_____	_____	_____
New Products (#)	_____	_____	_____	_____	_____

Remarks _____

Market investment: _____

Sales:_____

Net profit:_____

Production efficiency: _____

Stock sales:_____

Training conferences: _____

New Staff: _____

New products: _____

NOTE: You should make changes to this form to fit your own particular situation. For example, you may want to add columns, change year headings to quarters, or drop or add line items.

8

Tactics and General Strategies

There are old pilots, and there are bold pilots. But there are no old, bold pilots.

— Peter Drucker

By now, you have completed the first three letters of the four-letter SWOT formula: You looked at your Situation by gathering facts about your market and industry. Your Weapon resources are illustrated by your company analysis. Your Objectives were set out in the previous chapter. Now you are ready for Tactics and Strategies.

Some planners use the term strategy to mean the smaller or lesser daily actions. But unless this distinction is clearly spelled out, confusion is generated. And so for our purposes we will use both strategy and tactics interchangably. We will usually use the word strategy. (Webster defines strategy as "the science of military operations" and tactics as "the science of battle maneuvers." They really do mean about the same thing.)

The purpose of this section is to suggest some general strategy plans. In later sections, we will consider some more specific and detailed action plans. From this point on, we are talking about *doing* things, as opposed to gathering information, studying and reviewing.

EXPLANATION

The easiest way to begin planning strategy is to look at the business as being made up of several key parts, groups, or departments (even though one person may fill several or even all of the roles).

First, a company has a person or group that produces goods or services (or buys these). Second, a group sells these goods or services. Third, another group keeps records and finances the operation. These three activities are aided by three more people or groups: management (who coordinates the activities), technicians (who develop goods and services), and staff (who help in all in these areas). This totals six functioning groups.

We will look at some general strategy steps for each of those six groups.

There are several circumstances, conditions, or situations that usually face an entire company. Therefore these same conditions also, to a degree, confront each of the six individual functioning groups. The most common situations challenging a company are:

- A start-up or new product.
- Slow growth
- Fast growth
- Improvement needs (no growth)
- Adjustment/reaction needs
- Survival (hanging in there)
- A decline or reduction of operation
- Sellout, close-up, or failure
- Buyout, takeover, or expansion

Now we can simply match each of those conditions to our six groups. Then we can suggest some strategic actions each group might take as it faces these challenges.

The Strategy Matrix. This match-up of 1) department with 2) typical situations can be done by a chart, forming a matrix. We can enter a simple strategy suggestion for each group in each situation. These are typical choices. Your particular company may need to take different steps. We will show this for one fictional company with less than a hundred people, although the suggested strategy steps come from several real business experiences.

All this gives you two advantages: First, it lets you "dip your toe" into the strategy pool and get the feel of planning strategy to meet various situations. And second, this suggests some reasonable and practical tactics that you can plan to use, as is, or you can use the tactics as a starting point for suggesting other alternatives.

DEMONSTRATION OF GENERAL STRATEGY SUGGESTIONS

Group or Department

Situation	Producers	Sales	Finance	Mgmt	Technicians	Staff
Start-up	R & D + new products details	Check Market & planning	Presentation for funds	Plan and co-ordinate	Test R & D results	Stay small then grow
Slow growth	Introduce as items are available	Introduce as items are available	Funds by debt and equity	Find ways to build sales	Search to fill needs & wants	Select aggressive people
Fast growth	Push to keep up trends	Push but with logic	Stock sales to get funds	Push and grow with care	Heavy search action	Expand but with care
Improvement (no growth)	Test to find bet ter ways	Test to find bet-ter products	Find New $ sources methods	Study competitors & research	Training & more staff	Train current
Adjustment (reaction)	Outdo competitors' efficiency	Check competitors & outdo	Keep control & flexibility	Resolve to outdo competition	Copy good items & improve	Plan to grow or trim
Survive (hang in)	Study, copy, and improve	Protect market niche	Control & cut costs	Control costs & up sales	Buy available innovations	Trim to the minimum
Decline (reduce)	Cut dollars costs to produce	Push with idea,item niche	Cut dollars build control	Consoli-date jobs	Build results, cut costs	Trim, keep best
Close-up (sellout)	Stop building inventory	Let fade slowly, hold sum	Sell assets high	Trim & sell staff to buyer	Stop large in-vestment	Trim and give good notice
Buyout	Check product strength	Check market trends	Review assets profits	Assess strengths/ weaknesses	Assess, keep the best	Care, move slowly

NOTE: Nearly all the entries in this strategy matrix are action words. Strategy is action, not study or goal setting.

Here is a more in-depth review of the important information contained in this chart.

When the situation is a start-up or a new product/service introduction, a good strategy plan for production groups is to emphasize strong Research & Development plus detailed new product planning. Sales/marketing people will want to consider good market research and planning. Finance personnel will want to plan and present proposals for improving the financial situation. General management will want to emphasize careful, efficient planning and coordination. Technicians should emphasize R & D and testing. The staffing plan might be to stay small, but to grow as needed.

When growth is slow, production should plan to push product innovation and introduction. Marketing the same. Finance might plan to seek improved funding through debt and equity sources. General management might plan strong commitment to accelerating growth. Technicians might plan to keep looking for ways to fill customer wants and needs. Staffing might plan to be slow, selective and to seek aggressive people.

When growth is fast, all players should remember that these are heady, exciting times, but there is some danger. Production should plan to push for output, but also watch efficiency. Marketing should push and strike while the opportunities are available. Finance should aggressively seek funding. Management, too, should move aggressively, but with care. Technicians should institute a heavy search for innovations. The staff should expand, but with care.

When there is a strong need for improvement, production should seek better, more efficient methods. Sales/marketing people should test for customer wants and plan better marketing strategies. Finance might seek new funding sources. General management might study successful competitors and borrow more effective methods. Technicians might add training and increase research. Staffing people might improve staff training to build efficiency.

When the situation indicates an adjustment is needed, production should outdo the competition on efficiency. Sales should check competition and outdo them on marketing. Finance should stay in control but be flexible. Management ought to resolve to outdo competitors. Technical people should copy and improve on good items. Staffers should plan for both growth or reductions.

When the business' survival is at stake, production should study, copy, and find ways to improve efficiency. Sales should protect their market niche. Finance should control and cut costs. Management should control costs and work to raise sales. Technicians should buy available innovations. Staffers should be trimmed.

When declining or cutting back, production should reduce production costs. Sales should push new ideas, new items, and niche protection. Finance should keep dollar control and cut costs. Management should consolidate jobs. Technicians should build for better innovation, but cut costs. Staffers should trim their numbers but keep the best.

When closing up or selling out, production should minimize inventory investment. Sales should let the volume fade slowly, holding as much distribution and volume as possible. Finance should sell its assets to the buyer for the best possible price. Management should sell its staff to buyer, where possible. Technicians should stop any large investment. (It is not likely to be recouped.) Staffers should regroup and give good, long-term notice where possible.

When your company is buying out another company, production should check the seller's production strengths and weaknesses. Sales should check market position and trends. Finance should review assets, liabilities (debt and equity), profits, and ROI. Management should check overall strengths and weaknesses. Technicians should check seller's abilities (if any) and keep the best. Staffers should move slowly and carefully.

International considerations. Many parts of Europe are rapidly moving toward a market economy. This means several of the situations listed above will be very common for our firms, especially start-up situations and adjusting or reacting to new and strange situations. European product and service wants and needs may be similar to but not identical with those in the more mature markets of free enterprise societies such as the United States, Great Britain, France, and others. On the other hand, highly aggressive Asian markets in the Pacific rim, such as Japan and Hong Kong, will see more sophisticated fast growth situations and buy outs. Here the strategy listed may apply in general, but must be modified according to local customs. For example, Asian business practices require much more attention to human relationships, diplomacy, and face saving. In contrast to the United States, *how* a step is taken is often far more important that *what* is done. Procedure often supersedes substance.

Make your strategic plans, check them out with local business people before acting, and then move with care. Be ready for prompt adjustments. Managers in other lands may have some advantages, but U.S. managers often have been working in a competitive market longer.

STREAMLINED GENERAL STRATEGY FORM

Our situation is: (example, Start-Up) _____

general strategy plan for each department -

Production: _____

Sales:_____

Finance:_____

Management: _____

Technicians: _____

Staff: _____

Now you have set some general strategy action plans for your company. You should be starting to feel fairly familiar with the strategy, and be comfortable thinking along those lines. If so, you are in a great position to move aggressively and efficiently into good, profitable strategic action planning.

9

Will the Idea Work?

Who decides when even the doctors disagree?

— Ben Franklin

As a good planner, you have gathered facts about your industry, your company, and your resources. At least one and probably several of those items may be new ideas for products, services, or ways of selling. With all these in mind, you have decided on apparently reachable goals. Now you are planning strategic steps for using your weapons or resources to achieve those goals. But are your strategic plans for product, service, and marketing good enough to achieve your goals? Is your strategy feasible? Will your new product fly? How do you know? Here are some answers.

Feasibility studies or tests are fairly routine in most major, successful companies. Webster defines *feasible* as "probable, doable and successful." Feasibility tests will tell you which of several alternatives will most likely work well. And these studies can be small and low cost for the smaller or mid-sized company.

Your bottom line, of course, *is* the bottom line; profits. You will get those profits by selling good products or services. And, naturally, you will sell, and people will buy, only those goods and services desired by your market.

You make major gains by avoiding "production thinking." This is where someone says, "We don't care if the market wants red widgets, we like to produce green ones, so we are going to make green ones." They might also just as well add, "And we don't really care much if the market doesn't buy our green widgets." This sort of thinking is often the group's own worst enemy. It is not good management. Solution: be market oriented, not production oriented, and you will see more sales and more profits.

"OK, that makes sense," you might say, "but how do I know *which* product my prospective customers want?" Ah, there's the rub! But there are several simple answers.

The objective here is to give you some proven tactics for discovering whether your concept is practical and whether your customers want your new idea, or which of several is most favored. As usual, we will provide an explanation, a demonstration, and practical project forms for you to use.

There are at least three highly effective ways you can determine if a concept (product, service, ad theme, or other idea) is feasible. The idea is to learn what people like and therefore what they will buy. First, you can simply ask them. These days, most prospects aren't tongue-tied. They have plenty of opinions and they aren't slow to give them. Second, when you have a prototype, model, or sample they can see and use, you should learn *what* they like and don't like about it. And third, you can try selling the product in a small, typical test market, or (often nearly as useful) look at what people are actually buying in the normal market. In a way, that strategy lets others do the market test for you, at no cost. If and when these feasibility tests suggest adjustments, you will be wise to make the changes as best you can. Ignore the market roadsigns at your peril; follow the signs to success.

Here, we are talking about tests, done among a small, representative sample of 200 to 400 people. This is low cost, practical, minimal testing—mainly dipping your toe in the water, before diving in only to find it's just an inch deep. That hurts. Such small tests measure only a limited number of variables.

Testing minimizes the influence of any one salesperson. It helps all involved agree on all steps before starting, permits mid-course corrections but then assumes that the managers have the courage and confidence to follow the results, avoiding a mistake when the data is not favorable or moving forward on good results.

Why test feasibility?

1. Such tests simplify your life. They conserve and protect your capital, build corporate safety, personal security, sales, profits, and ROI. These tests help you avoid painful mistakes that can ruin a company.

2. Tests cut down on your guesswork. Major market analysts, including A.C. Nielsen, say that management judgment is right only about 50 percent of the time and only one project in five (about 20 percent) makes a profit. Feasibility testing lets you do your best to sort out the four poor concepts, find the fifth (the one worth expanding), and do it at a low cost, with in-house people. Remember, anyone can simply guess, spend money, and go broke. It happens to 200,000 firms yearly. Failure is easy; success takes work.

3. Feasibility tests are forgiving. With low-cost tests, you can make all sorts of mistakes and hardly be noticed. You can "start" many new ventures and try lots of new ideas cheaply, safely, and without fear of disaster.

4. Tests save you time, argument, indecision, risk, and delay. Tests put modern scientific methods on your side. Such methods have saved thousands of firms from failure and brought prosperity to thousands of others, generating billions in sales and profits.

5. Feasibility tests build efficiency. Done properly, they let you make much better use of capital. For example, if you have $100,000 available for a program, and use $10,000 to run a few small tests to find the best approach, you may double the impact of the remaining $90,000 to $180,000. Even if you only increase the efficiency by 25 percent, it gives you the impact of roughly $112,000, still a wise use of capital. And, after all, that is what managers are hired and paid to do: manage capital.

6. Good decisions are made for you. When you do a few tests, a good marketing plan is almost automatically made. Sound, practical decisions are clearly indicated for product design, package, price, premium, promotion, personal selling, physical distribution, publicity, or advertising. Now, all you need do is expand these into larger markets. You are a little like an airplane design engineer who has tested every part. You know that when you finally put it together, it will succeed. As it moves down the runway, you can casually get back into your car and go home. You don't even need to watch. You know it will fly.

7. Multi-billion dollar Procter & Gamble, often called one of the world's best run corporations, says, "We simply aren't rich enough to move without feasibility testing." And they use small programs to test just about everything—nearly all parts of the product and marketing strategy program. Tests are used by most of the world's best companies, with proven success. The methods you will find suggested here out-Japan Japan!

8. This system simulates, stimulates, clarifies, and communicates. Done right, it almost won't let you fail. Success is almost automatic. And this is true even if you don't follow these steps exactly.

"Hell, no. It's not worth the time, money, and hassle!" some say. And they might be right, based on their own past experiences. Many managers have done some testing and been disappointed.

Usually, they made one or all of these errors:

1. The test was not designed properly, and so gave useless or incorrect results.

2. The test was designed by someone who wanted to charge a large market research fee—far more than was needed.

3. The researchers promised (or the manager expected) miracles. They forgot that the test may simply show that they should *not* do something—and although they avoid disaster, they still complain about the costs of the test.

4. The results were taken personally. Often the test does not confirm the manager's prejudgment. It proves him wrong, and he gets angry.

Some resist testing simply because they enjoy the excitement of the risk. They *like* playing Russian roulette.

Management ego: "I don't want a feasibility test! After all, I'm paid for my good judgment. Tests substitute for my insight. Then, who needs me? I've been replaced by a system!" All that is a little like an aeronautical engineer saying, "I don't *want* to use that expensive test equipment to measure things. I'll just use my own judgment!" How would you like to fly on *his* airplane? The truth is that there are proven systems to help you avoid errors, point to success,and attain much more authority, productivity, efficiency, and clout! You become even *more* valuable.

Success case: A small family-owned-and-operated business was working out of the garage. They produced bottles of fabric cleaner, were growing slowly, and showing only modest profits. Then they teamed up with a small professional marketing group. They all agreed on doing some feasibility testing. They worked out short versions of the flow charts you see later, although the ones here are improved a bit. They tested some new names, products, packages, promotions, and prices.

Some bombed badly. These were abandoned. Then samples of the favored items were made and customer opinion was tested again. Now the prospective customers were very favorable. The program was expanded.

Today, those products, *Fantastik* spray cleaner, *Janitor-in-a-Drum* and *Spray 'n Wash*, have dollar sales that total in the billions and are among the leading fabric cleaners in the world. The family members are each multi-millionaires. In many other companies, similar steps were taken with various products and services. These simple feasibility tests helped generate major prosperity.

Remember, there are three major feasibility tests that are low in cost and should always be considered. These do not always fit all companies at all times. But at least one of these steps will be appropriate. The three steps are:

1. Test the idea or concept.

2. Test a model.

3. Test the market.

Each one costs a little more than doing nothing, but does a lot more toward building high profits. The remainder of this chapter will cover these three feasibility tests and explain them, demonstrate them, and then give you a practical project form to use.

HOW TO TEST THE CONCEPT

This step costs very little if done right, and it gives you a double advantage: First, you can become fairly sure that the whole idea makes good sense. Second, you discover whether or not the concept is attractive both to your company and your customers. If the answer is yes on both counts, you are pointed toward profits. Concept testing usually has five steps, although you need only use those that are within your budget.

1. Look at your company situation. Is the new program affordable?

2. Look at your market. Who is it? Who's the competition? Are we any better? Why?

3. If the first answers were positive, only now is it efficient to write the plan.

4. Do the key company officers agree?

5. Do savvy outsiders also like it?

These are gutsy questions, but now is the time to be hard-nosed, not after big money is invested.

DEMONSTRATION OF CONCEPT FEASIBILITY TEST

1.	Is the plan affordable?	Yes, if modest steps are taken.
2.	Market—Who will buy?	New managers, mainly.
	Who is key competitor?	W.J. Janes, Co, publisher.
	Why are we better?	Quality. Price. Display.

3. Has plan been prepared?   <u>Yes, first draft.</u>

4. Has management reviewed and
    OK'd it?   <u>Yes, with suggested changes.</u>

5. Do prospects like it?   <u>Yes, if adjustments made.</u>

HOW TO TEST FEASIBILITY IN USE

The use test takes a little opened-minded humility, but gives you even greater confidence, safety, security, and certainty of success. In step one you move out of the idea stage to a prototype, model, sample, or detailed pictures. In step two you show this product or service plan to potential users. In step three you make any requested adjustments. In step four you recheck opinions of the revised product and in the fifth step you plan the investment program (cash flow forecast and financial details).

DEMONSTRATION OF A USE TEST AND RESULTS

1. Prototype made?   <u>Yes. The cost is $500.</u>
                             <u>Production takes two weeks.</u>

2. User opinions?   <u>30% liked. 70% asked for changes.</u>

3. Adjustment made?   <u>Partly. But some too costly.</u>

4. Users re-checked?   <u>90% liked. 10% asked for changes.</u>

5. Budget plan made?   <u>All management and board approved.</u>

HOW TO TEST THE MARKET FEASIBILITY AT LOW COST

If you have conducted both of these tests, now you have both a proven concept and a proven product. The question now is: Can it be profitably sold? A small feasibility test market will tell you. Here you are making the largest test marketing investment, but you also have the most reason to believe that success is likely. This, of course, should be done only where practical, where the cost of the test is much smaller than the cost of a full-blown failure.

Looking below, you can see that the first step is planning the market program. A real campaign is run; results are measured or problems found. If necessary, changes are made and the program rerun until profits are satisfactory. Then, at step two, the program is expanded, perhaps regionally, nationally, or internationally. And this is done with confidence, since you now have a proven concept, a proven product, and a proven marketing program. Profits are *almost* certain.

DEMONSTRATION OF A FEASIBILITY MARKET TEST

1.	Planning:	Small, typical test market found
	Program run:	Marketing run Jan. 1-June 30
	Results:	No break even. Errors located.
	Adjust and rerun:	Changes made. Retest Jul. 1-Oct. 1
	Results:	Excellent profits.
2.	Expansion:	Move to N.E., U.S., then national.
	Plans:	Later, Canada, Britain, Germany
		Expand corporate stock sales

CONCEPT FEASIBILITY TEST

1. Is the plan affordable? _____

2. Market—Who will buy? _____

   Who is key competitor? _____

   Why are we better? _____

3. Has plan been prepared? _____

4. Has mgmt reviewed & OKed it? _____

5. Do prospects like it? _____

USE FEASIBILITY TEST

6. Prototype made? _____

7. User opinions? _____

8. Adjustments made? _____

9. Users rechecked: _____

10. Budget plan made: _____

MARKET FEASIBILITY TEST

11. Planning: _____

    Program run: _____

    Results: _____

    Adjust and rerun. _____

    Results: _____

12. Expansion: _____

    Plans: _____

Errors. We have seen two major testing errors by managers. First, no test at all (committing major investments based on judgment alone). And second, tests that are much too long, large, and expensive. Some managers become overimpressed and fall in love with market research. Or they become pushed, pressured, and seduced by a market research group that wants to make their fortune on one spin of the wheel and one project. This is very short-sighted, since such a firm can often make much more money by doing a number of small, successful profit building tests, over a period of years, rather than running one massive project that leaves the client discouraged, disillusioned, and uninterested in any further projects.

TESTING COSTS

Type of test	Low Cost	Medium	High Cost
Concept Test	$300.00	$1,000	$10,000
Days	5 days	30 days	60 days
Use Test	$500.00	$5,000	$20,000
Days	20 days	30 days	60 days
Market Test	$1,000	$20,000	$500,000
Days	30 days	60 days	180 days
Total Cost	$1,800	$26,000	$530,000
Days	55 days	120 days	300 days

Cost cutters. Naturally, since these are purely estimates and averages, actual costs may vary. You may wish to cut corners a bit, or elaborate on key points. You may choose to do shorter concept and use tests, but a longer market test. Or to design a program somewhere between the low and the medium ranges shown. Further, while the market test is by far the most costly, it often generates enough income to pay for most of its costs.

Other cost-cutting devices include grouping several projects from within the company (or working with another, noncompetitive firm). A feasibility concept test program can check out eight or ten new product ideas or proposed promotions. A use test can get opinions on several new items, services, or packages. A market test can introduce more than one new product or marketing program.

A well-planned, small, low-cost test can give more-than-adequate data, often just as good as large tests. You often do not need big, expensive tests. Don't get overwhelmed by statistical talk about standard errors and standard deviations or confidence intervals to justify a giant project, unless it is really needed.

Important note: This sort of a successful feasibility test record gives lenders or investors, dealers and distributors, suppliers and employees a very good reason to support your program aggressively.

Use this system. Yes, it takes time, money, patience, discipline, openmindedness, objectivity, scientific thinking and even a little humility to admit mistakes. But it pays off. Feasibility tests have brought billions into many corporations. At the very least they helped companies to avoid failure—and, often, to far surpass key competitors in the market.

Part II

Getting it Down on Paper

10

Making A Practical Marketing Plan

Find a need and fill it.

— Pete Small

A marketing plan is a written set of statements for efficiently moving those things to the user. The plan is a blueprint and a picture of your success.

When you make a good marketing plan, you enjoy several important benefits. First, and perhaps most important, you get a higher result on investment. You make your dollar work harder towards building increased sales and profits than that same dollar would work if it were invested without a plan. Second, you cut waste. Third, you build efficiency because you know what to do next. Fourth, you unify your team. All become involved and participate as part of the program. Fifth, you minimize risk, mistakes, and failures. Finally, you improve your company's progress and prestige—as well as your own. You build a feeling of confidence and personal support among your managers, bankers, and owners (and even among your suppliers and dealer network).

In summary, a good plan begins with a look at the Situation, inside the company and out. Then a check of Weapon resources: time, money and staff, skills, contacts, dealers, customers, reputation, equipment, supplies, products or services. Then you set your Objectives and list your Tactical action steps for product or service, price, package, premium, promotion, personal selling, physical distribution, and publicity and advertising. Finally, you set up a budget plan and time schedule.

Our purpose here is to cover those items in a rapid and practical manner, so that you can easily put them to work. We will review the Situation, Weapon resources, Objectives and Tactics. Then you will see a demonstration followed by a practical project form.

A simple outline will help you quickly see the whole thing in miniature.

```
TITLE page
EXECUTIVE SUMMARY page
SITUATION facts
WEAPON resources
OBJECTIVES/goals
TACTICS/strategy:
      Product or service
      Price
      Package
      Premium
      Promotion
      Personal selling
      Physical distribution
      Publicity and advertising
Budget plan
Test market plan
Schedule plan
Export market plan
Exhibits or supporting detail
```

The purpose of the plan is to generate efficient, profitable action. It is a set of usable, practical instructions, designed to insure that resources are properly applied and that everyone is singing from the same song sheet.

Length. Market plans can run from one brief summary page to over a hundred. But the ideal, for a stand-alone document, is twenty to fifty pages. If the plan is part of a total company strategic plan, then a two- to four-page marketing section may be sufficient. Large volumes of supporting documents can be attached as exhibits or under a separate cover. These seldom need to be part of the action plan.

Style. The plan should be short, practical, to the point, and workmanlike. Include appropriate and pertinent facts, brief goal statements, and action steps for tactics and strategy. Your plan should not be flowery, legalistic, prosy, or wordy. It should be clear and well-worded, but remember that it is not a piece of literature.

Here is a sample two-page marketing strategy plan, based on several actual small businesses that used similar programs with good success.

Title page: Company—<u>American International Consultants</u>

Address: <u>1016 42nd St, N.Y. 10305</u> Phone: <u>202/555-4050</u>

What: <u>Annual Marketing Plan</u> Date: <u>6/6/91</u> Place: <u>N.Y.C.</u>

Originators: <u>G. R. Able, C. S. Baker</u> Copy <u>#1</u> of <u>10</u>

Exec. Summary: <u>Our situation internally is slow growth or no</u> <u>growth over recent years. Externally, the industry is expanding and</u> <u>changing. We are losing market share. To correct this we are plan-</u> <u>ning improvement in product, package, premium, promotion, per-</u> <u>sonal selling, physical distribution, and publicity. All initiatives</u> <u>have been well checked in low-cost tests.</u>

INSIDE SITUATION: <u>Strengths: high skill of staff.</u>

Weaknesses: <u>Lack of capital.</u> Opportunities: <u>Possibly more effective</u> <u> use of skills via planning and 5 Ws.</u>

OUTSIDE SITUATION: 5 Ws—Who buys: <u>Mainly mid-sized NY</u> <u>service firms.</u> What: <u>They buy help in building profits or solving</u> <u>problems.</u> When: <u>Usually when circumstances have become serious.</u> Where: <u>Metro area.</u> Why will they buy from us? <u>A belief that we do</u> <u>a better job.</u> Why is our product better? <u>Because it is built on sur-</u> <u>veys to solve specific customer wants and needs.</u> Market size: <u>$175</u> <u>mill./year.</u> Trend: <u>Up 8% a year.</u> Opportunity: <u>Build awareness.</u> Potential: <u>$5 million sales a year.</u> Key competitor: <u>Parker Interna-</u> <u>tional.</u> Best source of customers: <u>Personal contact, media leads,</u> <u>reputation, talks at conferences, publications, client referrals.</u>

WEAPON RESOURCES: <u>Mainly a small budget plus sharp</u> <u>managers, good systems, good insight into market and efficient test-</u> <u>ing methods, dedicated staff, time, and good clients, reputation,</u> <u>contacts, and friends who believe in us.</u>

OBJECTIVES for next year: <u>Sales up 20 percent.</u>

TACTICS/strategies:(New action or changes planned; 8 Ps)

Product/service: <u>New sampler offer.</u>

Package: <u>New logo design planned.</u>

Price: <u>Special, half-price on introduction sampler.</u>

Promotion: <u>Sampler.</u>

Premium: <u>Free gold-embossed leather folder w/order ($50).</u>

Personal selling: <u>Local talks (NYC), visit selected prospects.</u>

Physical distribution: <u>Greater outreach—Europe.</u>

Publicity/advertising: <u>"A.I.M. Helps You Reach Targets."</u>

Media: <u>Mainly direct mail.</u>

Budget: <u>$100K budget for the next 18 months, 20% sales up pays out.</u>

Tests: <u>3 advertising themes, 3 promotions tested with prospect panel</u>

Test new logo design, market test Europe and sampler plan.

Export: Checking Germany, Spain, Poland.

Time Sched: Tests, first quarter Market manager helps introduce second quarter.

Exhibits: Detail on sampler, logos, premium, themes to test.

WORLD'S SMALLEST MARKETING PLAN Using SWOT

SITUATION: One fact, like, "Static sales"

WEAPON Resource: A small budget

OBJECTIVE: $100,000 sales increase next year

TACTIC/STRATEGY: Introduce a superior new product

(Note that the tactic or strategy is not an end in itself, but a means to an end. The situation and resource led to an objective. The objective led to the strategy. Keep that in mind and you will always find planning to be quite easy.)

MARKETING PLAN OUTLINE (Short form)

Company name: _____

Address: _____ Phone: _____

What:_____ Date: _____ Place: _____

Originators: _____ Copy #_____ of_____

Exec. Summary: _____

INSIDE SITUATION

Strengths: _____

Weaknesses:_____

Opportunities: _____

Other 5 Ws _____

_____

_____

OUTSIDE SITUATION

Strengths: _____

Weaknesses:_____

Opportunities: _____

Threats:_____

Other 5 Ws (Especially who buys what from whom and why) _____

_____

_____

WEAPON RESOURCES

(Budget, staff, skills, contacts, dealers, reputation, time, systems, equipment, inventory, systems, quality product/services, facilities):

_____

_____

_____

OBJECTIVES for next year:

TACTICS/STRATEGIES

(New action or changes planned) 8 Ps

Product/service: _____

Package:_____

Price:_____

Promotion: _____

Premium:_____

Personal Selling:_____

Physical distribution:_____

Publicity/ads:_____

Budget: _____

Export:_____

Time schedule: _____

Exhibits: _____

Please note that this is a short version. A good, comprehensive marketing plan with space for more complete entries would run much longer.

Leave blank any parts you can't answer. Perhaps ask others (such as marketing and advertising people) to fill in the blanks or suggest changes. Some items can be marked N.A., meaning "not applicable."

Use this general approach and you will find your market planning more profitable, easier, better understood by all concerned, and even (yes) fun!

11

Production Planning For A Superior Product

Ideas rule the world.

— Emerson

Your level of skill, efficiency, and design of goods and services often decides your survival. Your plan is what determines and controls your efficiency and design. Without careful planning, today's high speed machinery can turn out bad product at an alarming rate!

You benefit greatly from a good plan by avoiding both flawed or defective product (as well as avoiding production of the wrong or unsalable product). It also prevents producing product or services at excessive and disastrously high cost, which simply can't be recovered by selling price. Our economy is market driven, as is increasingly true throughout the world. Customers will not pay more for a brand that is virtually identical to lower-priced competitors. A moderate premium for a much-superior product, yes. But otherwise, customers are highly price conscious.

The aim here is to give you some useful production planning guidelines. We will discuss and explain them, demonstrate them, and then provide a practical production planning form.

The two keys to successful production planning have already been mentioned: the *right* product or service and the *right* price. Or, in different words, the proper design produced efficiently at low cost so a market price can cover costs and show a profit.

Efficiency. Since our economy is market driven, we prosper and are rewarded when we satisfy the customer at a reasonable price. If a production planner and manager can produce a product so efficiently that it can be priced lower than the competition, customers will reward that producer by buying the product. Clearly the action word is *efficiently* (meaning more or better goods or services are produced per dollar or per hour). Costs per unit are less.

Rewards. Some producers cry, "I don't see how my competitors can sell their products so cheap! They must be cheating!" Probably not. More likely, they have simply used good production planning and systems to operate more efficiently. Their costs are less. Their price is less, and they grab the market. That's good old human ingenuity and free enterprise at work. Efficiency is rewarded. If a managers or owners are willing and able to operate on a smaller profit margin than the competitor, they are able to price lower and win the market. (Discount stores and supermarkets are good examples.)

To design a product that customers want and will buy, consider these steps:

- Check your sales, advertising and marketing people. They often know their customers well.

- Check customer opinions, likes, and dislikes. Design products customers want, not what you want.

- Check competitors. What do they sell most? Least? Avoid the bombs. Improve on the winners.

- Check your dealers. What do they recommend? They see the prospects and competitors every day, and they know what sells. They aren't always right, but they usually are well-informed.

- Check your suppliers. They often have large research and development staffs who have improved products, materials, supplies, packages. Often this grows out of customer surveys and is checked with prospects. Suppliers are rewarded for generating improvements. And this costs you little or nothing.

- Check independent research and design services. They can often improve your product or service cheaper than you could do it yourself. They may even have something at a bargain price, or be able to suggest low-cost improvements.

Schedule production to match the marketing program. For example, product A might be set for promotion in months two and three. Thus you may want production and inventory to build up during months one and two, perhaps at the rate of ten thousand each month. Other products may have different time and volume patterns, as shown.

PRODUCTION PLAN

by Product, Volume (in thousands), and Month

Product	Jan	Feb	Mar	Apr	May	June	Jul	Aug	Sep	Oct	Nov	Dec
A	10	10	—	—	—	—	—	—	—	—	—	—
B	—	5	5	—	—	—	—	—	—	—	—	—
C	—	—	—	—	—	20	20	20	—	—	—	—
D	—	—	—	12	12	—	—	—	—	—	—	—

Control volume, cost, and inventory. Clearly, as production volume goes up, some economies of quantity set in, and unit cost usually drops sharply. The cost per unit is less when a hundred are made than when only ten are made. But three other factors raise costs:

1. *Total costs* are more to make a larger volume such as 100 than to make 10.

2. *The larger volume must be handled,* moved, and stored, which takes time, equipment, space, people, and money.

3. *Capital funds are now tied up in inventory.* Those funds, if borrowed, have an interest expense. They also might be more profitably used elsewhere.

The point is that you should calculate volume savings, but you must also measure these other costs of large quantities. When you add it all up, they will reduce expected savings on volume production. Ignoring this is a mistake amateur planners often make. (I did.)

Use just-in-time delivery and inventory control. If you plan your volume by product and date with care and accuracy, you can enjoy added savings. Thoughtful plans replace cash expense. You can and should schedule supplies to arrive "right on time" to be used in production. This minimizes the surprisingly high costs of storing and handling excessive supplies, as well as the cost of tying money up in materials inventory. The key here is to work closely with a good supplier who can deliver proper amounts at a precisely scheduled time. Suppliers, too, are watching their inventory.

Quality control is a vital part of production planning. First, have detailed and accurate knowledge of the product specifications. Second, be sure that the procedures produce according to those specs exactly. Make small test runs if this is practical. Third, review and track down points where flaws are likely. Fourth, review customer complaints and returned product to identify needed corrections. Fifth, make extra efforts to prevent flaws from occurring. Sixth, arrange for inspection points and sampling. Seventh, give quality control a very high priority. Low performance in this area by many U.S. companies has caused serious loss of market share, sales, profits, and jobs.

Material handling is a source of high cost when done improperly, but of major savings when done correctly. An easy way to plan good, efficient methods at little or no cost is to talk to your material suppliers. Often, they will gladly tell you how your competitors do it! Also, material handling equipment sellers will be glad to recommend various systems. But be careful: don't buy fancy equipment that performs beyond your needs. In a small firm, simple methods and equipment usually do the job best.

Storage, packing, and shipping plans are also major sources of costs or savings. Good programs can be obtained from the sources just mentioned, often at no cost. Test several methods and consider suggestions by the plant people who perform the functions every day. Offer a small incentive on volume handling and you will be amazed at people's ingenuity!

OVERALL PRODUCTION PLAN

STEPS	TIME (Weeks or Months)							
	1	2	3	4	5	6	7	8
Design surveyed	xxx	—	—	—	—	—	—	—
Design tested	—	xxx	—	—	—	—	—	—
Lab test	—	—	xxx	—	—	—	—	—
Use test	—	—	—	xxx	—	—	—	—
Blueprints, specs	—	—	—	—	xxx	—	—	—
Equipment ordered	—	—	—	—	—	xxx	—	—
Supplies ordered	—	—	—	—	—	—	xxx	—
Equip installed/ tested	—	—	—	—	—	—	xxx	—
Supplies arrive	—	—	—	—	—	—	xxx	—
Supplies stored	—	—	—	—	—	—	—	xxx
Production run	—	—	—	—	—	—	—	xxx
Production inventory	—	—	—	—	—	—	—	xxx
Product sold/ shipped	—	—	—	—	—	—	—	xxx

Note: The *xxx*'s might be specific dates and names of people doing these things. Notice how we ease into the production phase. A common error is to rush into manufacturing too quickly, before the homework is done. Result: lots of useless product. This can damage or destroy an operation. Note also that once all the pieces are in place, a number of steps can be taken concurrently. And finally, note that your product or service planning should probably cover these or similar points even if you have no manufacturing plant.

Here are two practical project forms for you to use. Others might include lists of your suppliers, equipment, skill people, outside support people, and inventory space by capacity for both raw supplies and finished product.

PRODUCTION PLAN VOLUME

by Product and Month

Product	Jan	Feb	Mar	Apr	May	Jun	Jul	Aug	Sep	Oct	Nov	Dec
_____	—	—	—	—	—	—	—	—	—	—	—	—
_____	—	—	—	—	—	—	—	—	—	—	—	—
_____	—	—	—	—	—	—	—	—	—	—	—	—
_____	—	—	—	—	—	—	—	—	—	—	—	—

OVERALL PRODUCTION PLAN

STEPS	1	2	3	4	5	6	7	8
Design surveyed	—	—	—	—	—	—	—	—
Design tested	—	—	—	—	—	—	—	—
Lab test	—	—	—	—	—	—	—	—
Use test	—	—	—	—	—	—	—	—
Blueprint, specs	—	—	—	—	—	—	—	—
Supplier review	—	—	—	—	—	—	—	—
Equip. designed	—	—	—	—	—	—	—	—
Equip. ordered	—	—	—	—	—	—	—	—
Supplies ordered	—	—	—	—	—	—	—	—
Equip. installed	—	—	—	—	—	—	—	—
Supplies arrive	—	—	—	—	—	—	—	—
Supplies stored	—	—	—	—	—	—	—	—
Equip. tested	—	—	—	—	—	—	—	—
Production run	—	—	—	—	—	—	—	—
Product inventoried	—	—	—	—	—	—	—	—
Product sold/-shipped	—	—	—	—	—	—	—	—

TIME (Weeks or Months) is the heading above columns 1–8.

Items that do not apply to you can be left blank, marked N.A., or replaced with a more appropriate step. For example, you may not include new equipment in your plans, but you will probably need supplies ordered, stored, and production runs. Also, some operations do not run on batch or job lot orders but, instead, run continuously. That calls for modification of the form.

The system applies to the service business, too, although a little modification is necessary. The steps might read: service designed, surveyed, use tested, support material prepared, service personnel recruited, trained, moved into test market, expanded into other markets, service modifications noted, modifications made, and tested.

The key is orderly planning. First, carefully integrating and considering steps that need to be taken. Second, putting these in the right order: steps taken prematurely or too late can generate waste. Third, recognizing steps that can be done concurrently, avoiding time loss. Fourth, avoiding too many actions at once, which can cause inefficiency. Fifth, integrating the production with the marketing action. Sixth, always relating action to time. And finally, putting the program into a few simple charts or tables that everyone can understand, again raising efficiency.

Follow these general guidelines, and you will produce the right product or service at the right time with high efficiency and low costs. That means you will be able to compete effectively in the market.

12

Financial Analysis: Planning For Profits

Common sense is the measure of the possible.

— Amiel

"Control your business, or it controls you," said Andrew Carnegie. When you use a few simple financial tools to analyze your business, you build both a plan and the control to work your plan.

The purpose of this section is to explain some of these tools, demonstrate their use, and then give you some practical project forms to use. We will also look at some important documents that can help you gain approval on a loan.

There are three basic financial documents that permit you to analyze, control, and plan. The first is the balance sheet. This simply shows you what assets the company owns and what liabilities it has. Liabilities include what the company owes to the bank and to owners. The second document is the profit and loss sheet (P & L). This shows what sales income the company enjoyed, less all costs, and then, what's left—a profit or a loss. The third key document is the break-even or payout and cash-flow chart. This is a running P & L. Often it shows losses in early periods, then a break-even period and, eventually periods of profit. Documents that help you get debt financing (a loan) or equity financing (by sales of stock) include a realistic forecast, expense forecast, list of suppliers, and repayment schedule.

Your balance sheet outlines your financial strength and health. Normally, the left side of the document lists the company assets. (That part is pretty easy. For the rest, you might find it helpful to think of the company as a separate individual, a person in its own right, rather than as you. That's why they call it a corporation.) The right side shows what the corporation (not you, but the company) owes to the bank (debt) as well as what the company owes to the owners like you (stock value or net worth).

Here's a very simple balance sheet for Company A. It contains only three separate numbered items in each category. This should help you get the feel of the document: what it looks like, what it means. (Many managers go through much of their careers making many mistakes because they are balance-sheet illiterates. Don't be one of them. This tool is not tough to understand, and it is extremely important.)

Company A

Assets Owned (in thousands)		Liabilities Owed (in thousands)	
Current assets		Current liabilities	
cash, etc.	$50	short-term loan	$20
Fixed assets		Long term liabilities	
bldg, equip.	60	long-term loan	50
Other assets			
intangibles	10	Net worth (stock)	50
Total	$120	Total	$120

Notice that the assets equal the liabilities; that's why it's called a balance sheet. What the company owns equals what the company owes. Another way of saying it is that whatever a company owns, it also owes, either to a lender or the owner. Total debt, long and short ($70), is subtracted from the total assets of $120. Whatever is left ($50), becomes net worth. This is usually equity ownership investment (stock) plus any earnings generated. In other words, this company is worth something. Sadly, this is not always true, as we'll see in a moment. Intangibles are things of value, but not cash in hand, such as goodwill generated by investments in time, money, and effort.

This balance sheet tells you that Company A is in pretty fair condition. It has enough cash ($50) to more than pay its short-term loan ($20), which could come due any day now.

Company B

Current Asset	$ 5	Short-term loan	$ 50
Fixed assets	25	Long-term loan	60
Other assets	40	Net worth	-40
Total	$ 70	Total	$70

Company B has a world of hurts. When you look at the figures, you easily can see why. Their current assets ($5) cannot begin to pay off the short term loan ($50). Their short-term debt is far too high. Worse than that, even if they used all their assets ($70) they couldn't repay their total long- and short-term debt ($110). This makes their net worth minus $40. This company is technically bankrupt. They can't pay their bills. This may be only a temporary situation, but right now, it is the reality the owners must confront. This is a picture you want to know, understand, and avoid.

Company C

Current assets	$ 100	Short-term loan	$ 40
Fixed assets	200	Long-term loan	100
Other assets	50	Net worth (stock)	210
Total	$ 350	Total	$ 350

Company C is in great shape. Their current assets ($100) can easily pay their short-term loan ($40) if it suddenly comes due. Their total assets ($350) could easily pay their total loans, short and long ($140). So you can easily see that they have a net worth of $210. Their short term loan is much less, in relation to their long term loan, than was true with Company B. These guys are really cooking! This is the kind of picture you should know, understand, and plan for your company.

These three examples are highly simplified. Later, the problems arrive in defining on some of the terms we have just seen, plus there are complex new line items that sometimes take a whole paragraph of footnotes to explain and even then are not always very clear. (For example, take a look at most any large corporation's annual report.)

THE PROFIT & LOSS STATEMENT (P & L)

The purpose of the P & L statement is to do just that; show profits or losses. The idea is to show sales and other income, then subtract major costs such as product, administration, selling expenses, taxes, and other expenditures. What's left is final or net profit. When we take income and subtract just the cost of goods sold, what's left is called gross profit.

This is a very important item, as you can quickly see. It's called gross because all the other operating expenses must be taken out of it to get to net profit. Naturally, the higher the gross profit, the more money is left to cover those other expenses. Like salaries. Your salary. Do you see why gross profit is so important?

Examples: Some companies have high product costs, so a very low gross profit remains. Other companies with about the same total sales, have only moderate product costs. That leaves a medium gross profit. Still other firms with the same sales, have very low product costs, leaving high gross profit. Here are three examples:

P & L DEMONSTRATION

	Low Gross	Medium Gross	High Gross
Sales Income (net)	$1,000	$1,000	$1,000
Minus cost of goods	700	500	300
Gross profit	$ 300	$ 500	$ 700
Other costs (minus)			
Admin. & research	200	200	200
Selling & Advertising	90	200	300
Net profit	$ 10	$ 100	$ 200

Clearly, there are many possible combinations. A change in any one number, up or down, sales in or costs out, affects the net profit or the bottom line. A low-gross company usually has less available for other expenses such as administration and selling. A high-gross company has more for these items.

When we increase the efficiency of any cost item, as your strategic plan usually tries to do, it has a favorable effect on the bottom line. And that is the objective of the whole enterprise, a good bottom line.

For example, if we produce more efficiently, at a lower cost, gross (and perhaps net) goes up. If administration, through people selection and motivation increases efficiency, again profits go up. If the marketing sells more or builds perceived value hence permitting a higher price per unit, sales income goes up and so does profit.

Everything relates. Pull one string, and something else pops up or down. Your plans should recognize this.

BREAK-EVEN EXPLANATION

Your break-even cash-flow or payout chart is one of your most important and useful financial tools. It helps you plan, control, and even secure equity (investment) financing, or debt (loan) financing, as we will soon see.

The break-even chart is simply a device showing estimates of income compared to expenses at different times. It is a sort of sliding P & L statement, moving along a timeline.

The purpose of the break-even chart is to show you when you can reasonably expect to break-even. In other words, when your total or accumulated income equals your cumulative costs. From then on (you hope) income will exceed costs and you will show a steady or growing profit.

The key differences between a break-even chart and a P & L statement are first, the break-even chart shows not one, but a series of income versus cost pictures. And second, the break-even chart shows cumulative income and compares this to cumulative expenses.

This is often called a cash-flow chart because, during the first few periods, the chart usually shows costs exceeding income and so a net loss. Money or cash is needed to flow into the venture, to cover those costs. But at some point, total accumulated income equals total accumulated costs. At that point there is no profit, no loss. The venture breaks even. In later periods, income exceeds costs. Now instead of pouring cash into the venture to cover losses, the venture provides profits, and the cash flows back out of the venture.

At least that's the theory. It seldom works exactly as planned. But nothing much happens *at all* unless there is a strategic finance plan. The break-even chart plan gives you insight, control, and a program for all to follow.

DEMONSTRATION OF A BREAK-EVEN CHART (in thousands)

Time Periods	1	2	3	4	5
Sales this period	$50	$100	$250	$400	$450
cumulative	50	150	400	800	1,250
Cost of goods this period	25	50	125	200	225
cumulative	25	75	200	400	625
Gross profit this period	25	50	125	200	225
cumulative	25	75	200	400	625
Other costs this period	75	100	125	150	150
(admin/sell) cum.	75	175	300	450	600
Profit (loss) this period	(50)	(50)	(0)	50	75
cumulative	(50)	(100)	(100)	(50)	25

The venture breaks even in the third period. (Periods might be a year, quarter, or month). In that period gross profit was $125 and all other costs were $125, so profit was $0.

But on an accumulated basis, gross profit through that third period was only $200. Other cumulative costs were $300, so to that point, the venture was still in the red by $100. However, in the next period there was a $50 profit, cutting the loss to date to only $50. In the last period there was another profit of $75, so now, the venture moves into the black with a $25 cumulative profit.

From a cash-flow basis, about the same figures apply. In the first period, the cash flow (or need to cover loss) was $50. The next period it took another $50. That equals a cumulative $100 loss. But at the third period there was no loss, so no further cash need flow into the venture. However, to that point the cumulative flow to cover losses was still $100. The profit in the fourth period means no further cash flow into the venture was needed, and part of the cumulative loss was paid off by a profit of $50. The fifth period paid it all off. This now produced an accumulated cash flow out of the venture of $25.

The major error in a break-even chart is that it all looks so easy and automatic. It isn't. Also, people making these charts are often dreaming, expecting far more sales and fewer costs than usually happens. The true key is to be realistic, even somewhat conservative. If anything, underestimate sales a bit, and overestimate costs a bit. Better to be surprised on the up-side than on the down-side. On the other hand, estimating sales *too* low will suggest that fewer needed funds be put into product, administration, and selling. This then lowers sales.

DOCUMENTS NEEDED TO
GET A LOAN (OR SELL STOCK)

A forecast of sales, costs, and profit or loss by time period is a key document for getting a loan. After all, if you were lending money to someone, you would want to know if they are ever going to make a profit and when. The break-even table we just reviewed is an ideal such set of information. Suggestion: to build believability, make three break-even charts—an optimistic, a pessimistic, and a realistic version. Surely you or anyone else would find such a presentation a bit more credible. Remember: nearly always, the key (and the key error) is the sales forecast.

An accurate list of costs, in detail, is also a highly useful document in gaining financing. This applies especially to many product and package components. The investor or lender wants to know that you have clearly thought out the hundreds of elements and obtained price quotes from reliable suppliers. Management hates surprises.

A repayment schedule, is also a key document. This shows how much repayment will be made each month or quarter to retire the loan. Or, a projection of profit distribution to stockholders might substitute for the loan repayment schedule. Ideally, you have both. Impress them!

A balance sheet projection is also very helpful. A lender (such as a bank) likes to see that there is some equity or stockholder investment, so that the lender is not all alone should trouble occur. The equity investor (that is, stock buyer) likes to know that the debt is not too large since, by law, debts must be paid before stockholders are paid. Both like to see a modest balance between debt and equity. And neither lenders nor owners want to see a negative net worth projected.

How the loan generates profits is another excellent list, document, or chart you might consider. This might simply be a list of reasons the investment will build profits, with special emphasis on sales building and cost control. Include a chart of profit expected for each time period.

You should specify how working capital will be used, by supplier and item for fix-up, inventory, equipment, payroll, advertising, and reserve. Lenders and investors don't want to feel that the funds might be used for a trip to Bermuda. (It happens!)

SOURCES OF FUNDING

You have two sources of cash money investment that you can use to operate your enterprise; debt (or loans) and equity (or stock owner-ship purchase). You get loans from a bank. You get equity stock purchasing through personal contacts, friends, associates, secondary contacts through friends and family and their friends and, very important, public stock offerings (although few of America's 15 million small firms are traded over the counter). Other sources include mortgages on your own assets like your home, equipment, or land.

A SIMPLE BALANCE SHEET

Assets owned by Company		Liabilities owed	
Current assets	$_____	Current liabilities	$_____
Fixed assets	_____	Long-term liabilities	_____
(blding, etc.)	_____		
Other assets			
Goodwill	_____	Net worth (stock)	_____
Others	_____	Others	_____
Total	$_____	Total	$_____

A SIMPLE PROFIT AND LOSS STATEMENT

Net sales income	$_____
Minus cost of goods sold	_____
Gross profit	$_____
Other costs	
Administration	_____
Research	_____
Sales force	_____
Advertising	_____
Other expenses	_____
Total other costs	_____
Net before tax	$_____
Tax expenses	_____
Net after taxes	$_____

BREAK-EVEN FORM

Time Periods

	1	2	3	4	5
Sales this period	_____	_____	_____	_____	_____
cumulative	_____	_____	_____	_____	_____
Cost of Goods this period	_____	_____	_____	_____	_____
cumulative	_____	_____	_____	_____	_____
Gross Profit this period	_____	_____	_____	_____	_____
cumulative	_____	_____	_____	_____	_____
Other costs this period	_____	_____	_____	_____	_____
(admin/sell) cumulative	_____	_____	_____	_____	_____
Profit (loss) this period	_____	_____	_____	_____	_____
cumulative	_____	_____	_____	_____	_____

If you understand these forms, how they were used in the example, and can apply them to your business (even in a simplified version) you have generated much more financial planning than many of your competitors. (At the very least, you'll be in a position to use the services of your accountant more effectively.) You should now be in a position to move aggressively toward greater success.

13

People Plan for a Winning Team

Morale is the soul of victory.
— Napoleon

"Does your executive candidate get on well with people?" is a question usually asked early in a selection process. The reason: people are often the most important single resource in businesses.

We will explain and demonstrate ways to plan a skills inventory, set up an organization chart, set job descriptions, establish an effective compensation and benefits statement, and use fourteen magic motivation methods. We'll also share some practical forms you can use to do all this.

Why are people so important?

1. *Action.* Without people, nothing much happens, even with lots of equipment. With people, a lot can happen, even with very little equipment. People make the difference, today more than ever because of much higher skill requirements.

2. *Budget.* Both today and tomorrow, they will cost more, so they are a large budget item. But it's more than just budget and action.

3. *Skills and abilities.* "Of all the business failures (last year), totaling over 300,000—80% of these, or a quarter of a million, were caused, not by inadequate capital, not by obsolete equipment or products—BUT BY POOR MANAGEMENT," observes Dunn & Bradstreet. Poor performance. If you improve performance, you increase your company's chances for success.

4. *Quality of life.* Good people management increases morale, spirit, and enthusiasm, so that one's career becomes part of one's quality of life. This stimulates productivity, action, creativity, and progress.

5. *Developing potential.* Surveys show people seldom use a fifth of their abilities. Most people are underutilized! Good management recognizes this as an opportunity for everyone. Good procedures can bring out talents that even the individuals didn't know they had. Result: Even low-cost people are more valuable because they do more and enjoy doing it.

An inventory of human resources is a wise planning step. It makes as much sense as an inventory of equipment and supplies, time and finances, since all these together represent your weapons or tools for progress. You may also be in for some pleasant surprises, since many people have skills that are not always recognized or used, but are available to you at no extra cost. Key elements in your inventory plan are a brief personal history, education, business experience, management experience, on-the-job training, experience in this business, personal goals, hopes and dreams, personal interests, hobbies, unused skills, and any special health precautions.

True, most of this is buried somewhere in the job application. But a special approach like this has several advantages for you: It is better focused, updates, refreshes memories, and builds morale. (In General Electric's Hawthorne, Illinois, plant, many personnel adjustments were made to raise morale. But in the end, managers discovered that just simple "concern for and interest in employees," alone and by itself, was the major motivator. This has been reconfirmed so often that it is now called The Hawthorne Effect.)

Here's a demonstration: A typical individual inventory.

Name and service time <u>Mary Rusche, 5 years with company</u>

Brief personal <u>Born and raised in Dallas. HS & college</u>

   life history <u>Born in Dallas area. Worked in NY 2 yrs. Married,</u> <u>no children. Husband; artist.</u>

Education <u>HS grad w/honors. 2 yrs. English maj.</u>

Business experience <u>Secy 1 year. PR writer, 1 year.</u>

Management Experience <u>Managed PR dept 1 year., 3 people</u>

On-the-Job Training <u>1- yr. program in print shop</u>

Experience here <u>Clerk, secy, print shop assistant</u>

Personal goals <u>Creative writing; to be an author.</u>

Hobbies <u>Painting, tennis, hiking.</u>

Unused skills <u>I like to write and do it well</u>

Health cautions <u>None; health excellent</u>

A simple organization chart is also a wise element in your people plan. It clarifies lines of communication and authority, and shows who reports to whom. People who can't draw such a chart are penalizing themselves and their group by making relations vague and uncertain. Good companies have a clear picture of their organization, one way or another. Photo charts are especially effective.

Here is a simple chart for an company of about fifty people. This one indicates the person, the basic duties and the size of staff. "Other jobs" means there might be other, miscellaneous occasional duties. The chart also identifies a part-time opening, for an export person.

This might be filled by one of the marketing staff, other officers, or staff members.

			Mr. A. President		
				Ms. B. Secy/Assist.	
Mr. C. Marketing	Ms. D. Production	Mr. E. Acct/Fince	Ms.F. Personnel	Mr. G. Tech	? Export
Sales People	Plant People	Records Payables	Employee records	Lab Also	(opened)
Advertise Publicity Complaints Other jobs	Warehouse Inventory Records Other jobs	Receiv'ls Inventory Control Other jobs	Process Orient Train Other jobs	Assist Plant Mgr. Other jobs	1/2 time
Staff of 25 people	Staff of 15 people	Staff of 1 clerk	Staff of 1 clerk	Staff of 1 assist	Staff ?

Job descriptions are a wise portion of the people plan. They should be prepared by the key personnel person, but cleared with the CEO and supervisor. The advantages are that the employee, supervisor, and everyone else knows what the person is supposed to do. Major mistakes in this area include:

1. preparing no job description at all,

2. making it too long, and including so many duties that these would be impossible for any one person to accomplish.

3. Using terms almost no one understands, even the writer, and sometimes appearing to be deliberately vague;

4. making no provision for new, unusual, collateral, or unexpected duties. Result: people say (or feel) "That's not in my job description, so I shouldn't be asked to do it."

5. relying on the job description to cover every tiny detail, as well as to serve as a substitute for a supervisor and as a motivator.

6. failing to get input from the applicant, incumbent, or supervisor.

The best job descriptions give a clear picture of duties and the reporting system. They show and explain the relationship with other people and, in that sense, might well include an organization chart. The person should not have to ask, "Where do I fit in?" Sentences are short and easily understood. Complex, esoteric words are avoided. Plain words are used. Remember, the applicant may not be a linguist or semantics specialist. Show the description to the applicant, incumbent, or others in the same field and be sure they understand and agree that no key items are missing and that the statements are reasonable. Don't get too long. One page (or even a half page) is usually enough. Here is a simplified example. In this case, it is applied to the export job opening we identified before.

Title	Export Specialist, half time.
Reports to	Company president.
Supervises	No one, at this time.
Relates to others	Work with department heads and others.
Key objectives	To help gain export profits.
Duties/responsibities	To understand the export program.
	To take & use export training.
	To help prepare export plan.
	To fit export efforts with company resources.
	To fit these with company goals.
	To analyze the company and industry.
	To help set goals, tests, marketing, production, finance, staff, outsider help, and general strategy.
	To help make things happen.
	Other related projects as needed.

A compensation statement should clearly indicate base salary plus fringe benefits, which sometimes approach the wages in dollar value. These fringes are increasingly important to employees and their families, and can be highly effective in motivating enthusiasm among workers. All compensation should be spelled out in some detail. If competitively favorable, then most of this might be in an employee booklet or orientation handout. That way, employees can see it, read it, understand it, refer to it, and take it home so the family can appreciate it, too. Many people don't realize the value of their total package, until it is added up for them.

Here is a typical compensation statement. Details are spelled out on the following pages. As you can see, there is little room for misunderstanding. These need not be as rich as those shown, although, psychologically and strategically, the company is wise to show at least something in each category.

Position	Export Specialist.
Salary range	$20,000 to $40,000.
Salary reviewed	Every 6 months.
Overtime	No pay, unless over 10 hrs/wk. then 125% of hourly rate.
Travel pay	None other than expenses.
Bonus/profit share	Varies w/co profits. 5% of pay.
Pension/retire	This is part of profit share.
Special awards	Varies. Usually luxury trips.
Vacations	2 weeks paid. 3 wks after 10 yrs.
Insurance	Extensive life & health.
Training	Part fully paid. Some half paid.
Day care	Arranged with nearby source.
Release notice	Two months notice (pay).
Relocation help	Stay in co., or help look outside.

Fourteen motivation methods that have proven to be highly effective might be considered as part of your people plan. Encourage officers to try these for a month. You will be surprised, and you'll start beating your competition.

1. Extend new challenges, such as the need to export.

2. Let people help set their own goals. (They stretch.)

3. Minimize fear and threats. These are demotivators.

4. Don't depend entirely on money. Psychology is stronger.

5. Show respect. It's one of the world's major motivators.

6. Meet and work together to solve problems. It stimulates.

7. Assign work that helps people reach personal goals.

8. Stimulate both heart and mind, not just mind alone.

9. Delegate. "You are V.P. in charge of _____."

10. Coach. "Together we'll solve this rascal!"

11. Communicate. "Modern management's major mistake is miserable communications." — Drucker

12. Let 'em run something. Be their own boss on a project.

13. Reward through recognition, certificates, and cash.

14. Recognize initiative and encourage it.

INDIVIDUAL SKILLS INVENTORY

Name and Service Time_____

Brief personal history _____

_____

_____

Education _____

Business experience _____

Management Experience _____

On-the-Job Training _____

Experience here _____

Personal goals _____

Hobbies_____

Unused skills_____

Health cautions_____

BASIC ORGANIZATION CHART (Show titles and names)

_____
President

_____
Secretary

Marketing	Production	Accounting	Personnel	Technicians
	Sales	Plant	Records	Lab

JOB DESCRIPTION FORM

Title:_____

Reports to: _____

Supervises: _____

Relates to others: _____

Key objectives: _____

Duties and responsibilities:_____

_____

_____

Other projects as needed: _____

Remarks:_____

COMPENSATION STATEMENT

Position and date:_____

Salary range: _____ From $_____ To $ _____

Salary reviewed:_____

Overtime pay: _____

Travel paid:_____

Bonus/profit share:_____

Pension/retirement: _____

Special awards: _____

Vacation:_____

Insurance:_____

Training: _____

Day care: _____

Release notice:_____

Relocation help: _____

Remarks:_____

PEOPLE MOTIVATION PLAN

Challenges:_____

Self-set goals:_____

Fear elimination:_____

Psychological strength:_____

Respect shown: _____

Meet/work together: _____

Work to your goal:_____

Stimulate heart:_____

Delegate:_____

Coach:_____

Communicate:_____

Your own project: _____

Recognition: _____

Initiative: _____

Remarks:_____

Use these strategic people plan steps and forms to help generate a dynamite organization. You will find you can move far ahead of your competitors, at little or no extra cost.

14

Outsider Plan

Providence favors those with the most resources.

— Napoleon

We all depend upon others outside our own group. Outsiders have certain skills and abilities that we don't have, and the fee is often worth the value provided. We all freely use the services of a teacher, clerk, barber, dentist, doctor, mechanic, banker, plumber, pilot, trash man, and many others without giving it a second thought. Yet many managers forget that there are dozens of business professionals available to help—and most of these are either free or low in cost. Managers who make good use of available, economical resources save themselves from expense, stress, and mistakes. They often gain major advantages over their competition.

Our objective with this section is to explain and demonstrate some of the most typical low-cost resources available to managers of small and mid-sized firms. You will find many are familiar, while others will be new or will remind you of forgotten sources. The demonstration will show how these can be used. Then we will provide a practical project form for you to plan your own outsider help program.

We'll look at the real costs of using resources and some guidelines for wise application that will get you more results per dollar than your competitor may be getting. The key sources we will review are your accountant, lawyer, banker, supplier, business friends, technician, ad agency, chamber of commerce, consultant, tax service, board of directors, trade associations, service club, realtor, SBA, SCORE, SBI, SBDC, college seminars, industry workshops, library, college instructors, bookstores, credit rating services (like Dunn & Bradstreet), publicity agent, personnel employment agency, travel agent, the U.S. Dept of Commerce, State Department, EXIM bank, and many others that above sources can recommend.

Here are some general guidelines, that apply to almost any resource you might use. Employ these and you will generally get high value per dollar or hour invested.

1. Recognize that these resources exist and are usually readily available. Know where the nearest ones are.

2. Know their approximate range of abilities and stay in that area. Ask a banker for advice on finance, not on marketing.

3. Don't be afraid to contact the resource. It costs nothing to ask. A short phone call may do it. The person may not be able to help you, but might know who can help. That's valuable.

4. When you visit, clearly define both your problem and your goal. This will save a lot of time and get you faster results.

5. Try to cover the who, what, when, where and why in their response. The 5 Ws. The fee. Sometimes the how.

6. Remember that the real cost of using these outsiders is their fee plus your time plus the cost of mistakes from poor advice; use your resources with some reservation and with care.

Your accountant or auditor is, according to recent surveys, the one outsider used more frequently than any other. Some firms visit with their accounting service professional every week or so. Managers make two common mistakes in working with this resource. First, they forget that the accountant often recognizes things in the figures that point to dangers or opportunities—places to economize or steps toward greater progress. Too often the manager looks on the accountant as purely a number cruncher. The manager should ask the accountant if he or she sees any clues that would help improve profits or management efficiency.

The second error is the flip side of this—expecting *too much* from the specialist. Few accountants are executive or management experts, and don't pretend to be. Keeping records and counting numbers is one thing, managing resources efficiently is quite another.

Your lawyer is a good source of advice and insurance against legal problems. A lawyer should be consulted when any major project is planned or even in small, new programs where there might be the slightest question of legality. For example, a new marketing program: don't ask the lawyer to design the strategy, but to advise you on it's legality.

Your banker can be a good friend, business associate, and advisor on finance. The recommendations are usually free. Ask him or her to look at your financial statements and forecasts. He sees many such items from other companies, both good and bad, and will often be quick to spot a potential problem before it gets serious. Such an ally is also more likely to assist you with a loan or other financial help, if needed.

Suppliers can offer a wealth of information. They sell to many other customers and they know what the smart operators do. Perhaps those managers have long ago solved a problem that you may be facing right now. Suppliers are usually glad to share this information with you, at no cost, so you don't need to reinvent the wheel.

Business friends can be another good source of advice. You will be wise to join a group, get to know a few local (noncompetitive) professional managers, then select some you respect; have lunch with them occasionally. In time, you will build friendships of men and women you can ask for (and offer) advice on a wide range of subjects. You'll be getting counsel from successful people that you trust, and the advice is likely to be pretty good. And free.

Technicians are expensive. But some of your men or women business lunch friends may well be a current or former engineer, architect, economist, or chemist. Your professional/social relations can sometimes ripen to the point where you both feel comfortable in asking technical questions. You might even bring one of your people to the lunch and discuss problems and solutions.

Advertising agency officers often get to know their clients quite well. This is good for both parties. It saves time for everyone and leads to more efficient programs, plus an enthusiasm that can generate that little extra plus in the marketing strategy. Agency people often work on market plans for many clients and pick up methods that can effectively be translated to different products and other clients. Many agency people are marketing specialists, yet their advice can sometimes be had for the price of a lunch or dinner.

Your local chamber of commerce represents two major resources. First, it is a source of business friendships, and a way of meeting good people in the nearby community, people with similar interests, rather than only through the golf course or bowling alley. Second, your chamber often has economic departments, or people very familiar with local conditions and statistics, as well as various other services available at little or no cost.

Management consultants can be excellent sources of advice and information on an occasional basis. The great advantage is that they usually offer a wide scope of training and experience. After a few years, there is hardly a problem they haven't worked on, perhaps many times. They see what works and what doesn't. They become very practical. (Obtaining free or low-cost advice from consultants is likely to be difficult.)

Your local tax service can provide tax advice on an as-needed basis. Their help can often save you expenses well in excess of their fee. Ask your other contacts (lawyer, banker, business friends) to recommend a good commercial tax service.

The members of your board of directors are not exactly outsiders. In many cases, much of the board is made up of company executives. Major mistakes made with company boards are appointing uninterested or unqualified people, and not using the talent and knowledge available from board members, often out of fear that they will try to take over operation of the company. That is rarely their desire. Most have more than enough to do. Further, if they are large shareholders, they can influence control anyway. It is best to become close associates and let them be friendly advisors.

Trade associations are one of the greatest sources of information, yet one of the most often ignored. Nearly every industry has some kind of association. These usually publish monthly or quarterly journals, often full of good industry information and advice. Further, an inquiry to their head office can get you back issue articles on almost any industry subject, usually at low cost. Such annual industry reviews can become your industry analysis, saving you thousands of dollars in time.

Service clubs such as The Lions, Rotary, Shriners or Kiwanis are excellent sources for meeting other company managers, executives, or specialists. Properly developed, through lunches, sports, cultural events, or community service projects, these can lead to valuable business friendships.

Your realtor is not the sort of person you may wish to contact very often, but you will be wise to know at least one or two. Realtors can be a good source of news about better locations, trends in the field of facilities, and what others in your area are doing.

The SBA, or Small Business Administration, is another excellent source of information. They have many fine videotapes on various management fields (usually available on loan at no cost), and they publish several dozen business and management booklets for $1 or less; they can help you with important, long-term financing, one-to-one business counseling, and management training workshops each year. All of this is available at little or no cost.

SCORE, or the Service Corps Of Retired Executives, is a program sponsored by the SBA. These are former owners and managers of their own businesses, volunteering to help small enterprise owners solve their problems. There is no charge. Many of these SCORE people are fairly well off; they know how it's done. They normally counsel for about an hour although they will be glad to do this several times, if you wish. SCORE is the world's largest management consulting organization; it can be contacted at the SBA office and, in many cases, will come to visit your business. SCORE also puts on Prebusiness Workshops in most states, programs best for start-ups or businesses with just a few employees.

The SBI, or Small Business Institute, is a program run through a number of colleges in each state. The colleges will, on request, send a team of two or three top senior college business students, supervised by an experienced college instructor, to help a small company. They study the firm for a few hours each week and then write an analysis or business plan. This often runs from fifty to a hundred pages, represents 100 man hours and would cost $5,000 or more if purchased from a consultant, but it is free. The students get course credit, and usually call this experience the highlight of their college training. A few months later, these same students graduate as entry-level executives, so they are not exactly amateurs. This program is sponsored by the SBA. It is not as good for start-ups as for on-going mid-sized firms.

The SBDC, or Small Business Development Center program, is also run through business colleges. The SBDC will provide top senior graduate business students and professors for short-term, intense counseling. Often this involves sophisticated statistical computer program analysis. This program is best for mid-sized businesses of fifty to five hundred employees. There is no charge.

College and industry seminars are often offered in nearby facilities. They are usually announced by mail, radio, or newspaper ads. They are generally well planned, polished, and professional, with good up-to-date information on special subjects (like marketing, motivation, finance, or export) at a price of $50 to $200 for a one-day session. A bargain, if it solves a real management problem.

Credit rating services (like Dunn & Bradstreet) can save you far more than they cost if your receivables and collectables are a problem. Many firms have been driven into bankruptcy by extending too much credit to the wrong customers.

Bookstores and libraries offer you access to some of the world's best business advice. See what these sources have to offer. Good business books represent one of the most cost-effective problem-solving resources.

College business instructors are often willing, knowledgeable, and experienced in management consulting. They are usually available on short notice and at moderate cost. Be sure to check references; quality varies widely.

Your publicity agent may be your advertising agency, but not always. Increasingly, companies are finding that important awareness, image, and credibility can be generated using good publicity, resulting in major sales. Good public relations can also increase the impact of advertising and other marketing activity like personal selling or promotions. It can be a major help in new product or new service introductions. While this service is not cheap, it is often worth many times the cost.

Personnel/employment agency. Your people are often your most valuable asset, yet many companies try to go it alone in recruiting and screening top-quality employees. A good agency can provide value far in excess of the cost.

Travel agents can speed up flight, hotel, and auto rental reservations, as well as find lowest priced deals or specials for traveling. A change of a few hours can sometimes save hundreds of dollars. There is no charge; agents get commissions from the suppliers. Yet some managers or secretaries spend valuable hours on the phone making their own arrangements, often paying higher rates.

Finally, specialists at the U.S. Department of Commerce, the U.S. State Department, major foreign embassies or consulates, EXIM bank, and larger local banks can provide key information for profitable exporting. This includes finding markets and prospects, handling forms, shipping and redtape, all at little or no cost.

DEMONSTRATION OF A PLAN FOR OUTSIDER HELP

Accountant	Clues to avoid problems, build efficiency.
Our lawyer	Check legality, especially on new projects.
Our banker	Check financial statements for problems.
Suppliers	Information on how we can make better progress.
Business friend	Advice on a wide range of subjects.
Technicians	Help resolve technical and production problems.
Advertising agency	Help make marketing plan more effective.
Local chamber of commerce	Meet people, advisers, get economic data.
Consultants	Offer proven advice on tough problems.
Tax service	Help cut taxes more than cost of service.
Board of directors	Use wide variety of skills & experience.
Trade associations	Summary of industry information and trends.
Service clubs	Meet other managers, executives, specialists.
Realtor	Spot new location opportunities, trends.
SBA	Check for better financing, management information.

SCORE	Review new plans and start-up methods.
SBI	Major research to find new customers.
SBCD	"What if" financial print-outs. Seminars.
Private seminars	Current methods, advanced management trends.
Credit rate	Check receivables. If low, check credit group.
Books	Improved management methods to raise profit.
College professors	Example: production engineer to check plant.
Public Relations Agency	Review new public relations proposal.
Employment agency	Too much turnover? Check for good steps.
Travel agency	Too much time setting up trips? Streamline.
Export agency	Need export sales? Check Commerce, State.

OUTSIDER HELP FORM

Accountant:_____

Lawyer: _____

Banker: _____

Suppliers: _____

Business friend: _____

Technicians: _____

Advertising agency: _____

Local chamber of Commerce: _____

Management consultant: _____

Tax service:_____

Board of directors: _____

Trade Associations: _____

Service clubs:_____

Realtor:_____

SBA: _____

SCORE: _____

SBI:_____

SBDC:_____

Seminars: _____

Books:_____

College professors:_____

Credit rate: _____

Publicity agency:_____

Employment agency: _____

Travel agency:_____

Export agency: _____

America became great because we used our resources. Don't forget to do the same for your business. The wise manager considers all of these resources and uses at least some of them.

15

Time Plan:

Powerful Secrets That Work

They'll forgive you for being late before they will for being wrong.
— Kettering

Time is one of your most valuable resources, and sometimes the most valuable one. Occasionally, timing is everything. Yet few managers know the many little tricks for using good planning to put time on their side. Such planning can double your effectiveness per day and help sell your plan.

Here we look at time as a resource, how to plan it, and how to find more of it to produce profits or just enjoy.

We will see that time is vital. Management of the past and present often becomes almost obsessed with it. A sense of time can motivate, focus efforts, and get more done per hour. Scheduling with a time plan can boost employee output, favorably impress investors, and increase company efficiency and profits. All this often begins with setting priorities, as well as knowing how to time or coordinate so that action occurs at the right moment. You will see a set of timely tips plus a time planning form that you can use.

Situation. Time is vital and critical to you for several reasons. First, as Ben Franklin said, "If you value life, then value time, for that is what your life is made of." Your time is your life, to use or enjoy.

Second, time is a major function of your career. Almost no one is an instant success. As singing star Tony Bennett put it, "After working hard for twenty years, all of a sudden I was an overnight success!" Time plays a major role is your progress and your prosperity. It can play a bigger role if you know how to use it.

Third, time is a major corporate resource. You pay people by the hour, week, or month. You are buying their time, and what they can do in that time. You are also selling or investing your own time. But, no matter how skilled a person may be, it is all for naught if time is managed poorly.

Fourth, time is vital because you not only schedule it daily on your desk pad, but you can also use it as a business management strategic plan that coordinates and unifies internal action and gets more done per day.

Fifth, good time management, planning, and scheduling impresses prospective investors (such as lenders or stock buyers). They usually have a keen awareness of time. After all, interest rates or profits mean nothing unless expressed in terms of time. A thousand dollars profit is not much if we are talking about a year. But, per minute or even per day, it begins to look like real money.

Weapon resources are twofold: 1) time itself, as a raw material and 2) a knowledge of or a system for using it. The program is often the key. Astronaut Neil Armstrong said, "If I were in space and had an emergency indicating I had only ten minutes to live, in order to save myself, I would spend the first three minutes gathering my facts. The next minute, I would be doubly sure I knew what I wanted to accomplish and knew what I was doing. And the last six minutes I would spend doing it." Now that's a ten-minute time plan that could be lifesaving.

Managers have been obsessed with time over the centuries as indicated by innumerable quotes and slogans.

In times of peace prepare for war.
— Machiavelli

Make hay while the sun shines.
— old rural saying

Let the time that makes you homely, also make you wise.
— Jacob Parnell

Timing has much to do with winning.
— Vince Lombardi

Use time in proportion to the investment.
— Senator Richard S. Budd

Good meetings avoid pouring tons of time down the proverbial rathole.
— Lakein

Assure the short run or there will be no long run.
— Peter Drucker

You can't change the past, but you can change the future.
— Ted Turner

Avoid paralysis by analysis.
— Peters and Waterman

Things take time. You can't get a baby in one month by getting nine women pregnant.
— billionaire Warren Buffett

The difficult we do immediately; the impossible takes a little longer.
— marketing slogan

Delays arranged while you wait.
— Bennet Cerf

Our *objectives* here, as stated in the purpose paragraph, is to make a time plan and put time to better use.

Your *tactics* for your strategic time plan should include these eight steps: generating a sense of time; setting priorities; focusing on MBO; using time schedules to sell and motivate employees; impressing investors; pouncing at just the right moment; using timely tips; and, finally, scheduling who does what, when, where, and why. Let's see how you can take each step.

1. *Generating a sense of time* starts with your own personal point of view. If you are convinced that good time planning and management can pay off for you and your company, begin by using many of the following items. Tell others about these. Show them how this will make them more valuable employees, help them get more done in less time, reduce stress, lead to rewards, and help them reach personal goals. Convince one or two and others will follow. Then hold a meeting and discuss the idea (include demonstrations). Encourage others to try their own time plan.

2. *List projects to do and then set priorities.* The easiest way is to take a moment at the beginning of the day or assignment. Simply list everything that needs to be done. Let one item remind you of others. Use a checklist, if needed. As you go along, put a circle in front of each item. Then go back and put a number or letter A, B, or C in each circle. Those are your priorities.

    How do you decide on a priority? Most people have trouble deciding on just what is really important. One easy way is to use two factors: 1) the value of the project to you, the boss, or the company and 2) the lead time involved. Projects with high value and long lead times should be done (or started) first. Give them an A. Projects with low value and short lead times are usually C priorities. Projects with moderate value or lead time, get a B.

Here's a chart that might help.

Priorities

	Long lead	Medium lead	Short lead
High value	A	B	B
Moderate value	B	B	C
Low value	B	C	C

The moment you do this, your efficiency level goes up, be cause you will be doing first things first, and putting high value, long lead time activities into the system soon enough to come together at the right time. What's more, your stress level usually drops, because you are not facing all the projects at once. Life is hard, by the yard, but by the inch, it's a cinch.

3. *Use time to focus on MBO,* or management by objectives. Priorities can be set for each of your objectives. This tells you what's important. Now, attention, time, and effort will be aimed at these top goals. They will be done first. You are managing your resources according to the objectives of the project or company.

4. *Use scheduling to sell and motivate employees.* See that everyone has a schedule. Now that you have established priorities for your goals and decided what needs to be accomplished first, second, and so on, the team can see the plan. Employees become far more enthusiastic about a plan when they understand it.

   At Valley Forge, George Washington discovered that even the most distressed troops became much more dedicated when they understood *why* they were fighting and what they were trying to accomplish. This message unifies, focuses effort, and gets everyone pulling together. During World War II, fifteen million American troops saw a beautifully produced weekly movie series called *Why We Fight.* It had a great unifying and motivating effect.

   Schedules have a motivating influence on most people. Be sure your team members have a copy of your schedule, showing their names and times. Many people have a compulsion to take the specified steps at the given time, but this is not really necessary.

   In many ways, we are creatures of the clock and calendar. This is especially true when we know that others are aware of the obligation, intend to do their part, and are watching to see that other people do theirs. As Drucker often says, "What gets scheduled, gets done." Clearly, time schedules motivate people.

5. *Use time schedules to impress investors.* They like to see that managers know what steps to take first and second. They like to see priorities, to know when things are going to happen, and that time has been planned. Most investors have been burned by putting money into projects that never happened because action was not scheduled correctly. They are

also anxious to know when they can expect profits and income. Show them the schedule and indicate what funds are needed and when. Now the investor becomes more directly and personally involved.

6. *Know how to wait.* There is a time to act and a time to avoid action. As the old poker song goes, "Know when to hold and know when to fold."

Smart timing can overcome many problems (even weaknesses or a major lack of resources). The sharp operator gets time working for him. He waits until the great stone wall is starting to crack, then gives it a gentle push and, to the amazement of his co-workers, it falls with a crash. Good timing, however, takes patience, discipline, and self-control.

7. Here are some timely tips to help you make smart use of your time:

   ● Everyone wants some of your time. Give this wisely. Especially your most productive hours.

   ● Begin with a list of things to do. Then give each item a priority, like A, B, or C.

   ● Be sure the A's are high value or need a long lead time.

   ● Mark the most essential item with a star.

   ● Now dig in; do first things first, one thing at a time.

   ● Try to work on toughest items at your best time.

   ● Don't give in to the temptation to do the easy things first.

   ● Remember, your greatest results come from your top priority items.

   ● Feel free to reorder your priorities as needed.

   ● Don't waste time traveling if a phone call will suffice.

   ● When you are delayed (at an airport, for example) have things to do.

   ● If a phone call gets too long, say "I have a call waiting."

- If the phone interrupts you too often, go to another desk.

- Be good to yourself. If you do a tough job, do an easy one next as a reward.

- Plan for interruptions. Expect it. This cuts stress.

- Get away from it all occasionally. Breath. Relax. Rejuvenate.

- Avoid irrelevant items. Don't take on the world's problems.

- Make big use of the round file. Toss junk quickly.

- Route items and delegate. Don't get overloaded.

- Don't let people dump their problems on you.

- Beware of time thieves who chat. Say, "I'm on a deadline."

- Try to start with a time limit on meetings, and keep it.

Here's a practical time schedule plans form that should be part of the strategic business plan you give to employees or investors.

TIME PLAN: NEXT THREE STEPS

WHO	DOES WHAT	WHEN
1.		
2.		
3.		

This may look pretty simple, but it has many advantages, as indicated above. Most strategic planners forget this. But plans that win acceptance from employees, company officers, and investors usually do have a good time schedule.

16

Export Plan:

The World Is Your Oyster

All people are one, under the skin.
— Anton

The U.S. represents only about 5% of the world's population. Domestic firms are missing 95% of the people. Today, right now, this year, American business faces new threats and new opportunities in the export area. Wise, aggressive U.S. firms will see many millions in new sales and profits. Less wise, less active firms will see much of their business taken away. It has already happened to some. We all face the stick-or-carrot situation.

This section will help you dodge the stick and enjoy the carrot. We will look at ten steps that a small or mid-sized company can take to improve sales and profits through exporting. We will explain and demonstrate each, then give you a practical project form to help you plan your own efficient export program.

Your best steps are to develop a small, simple plan for company self-analysis, industry fact gathering, goals, tests, production, marketing, finance, staffing, outsider help, and general strategies. All are important, but the keys are usually your own company's ability, plus your understanding of the unique opportunities and methods in a foreign market and use of outside experts, particularly the U.S. Department of Commerce, which provides a world of help for exporters, free or at low cost.

TEN STRATEGIC EXPORT PLANS EXPLAINED AND DEMONSTRATED

1. *Company self-analysis plan.* Since you should not consider exporting until you have at least a moderately successful domestic operation, the first question is, "How's business?" Are you showing a profit? Good trend? Do you have an exportable product? Concrete or haircuts may not "translate" well. Manufactured items fit better. What are your strengths and weaknesses? Staff skills and time? Here are simplified examples of two firms.

	Favorable Company Situation	Unfavorable Company Situation
Profit level and trend	Good. Up.	None. Loss growth.
Exportable product	Yes. Can ship.	No. Service.
Strengths	Superior item.	Same as local.
Ever exported?	Little. Canada.	No.
Staff skills for export	Some. Will train.	None.
Staff time for export	A little.	Little to none.
Advisors available	Know some.	None in our town.
Exporters known	A few.	No exporters known.

2. *Industry export fact plan.* This can be highly important. Export success or failure usually rides more on good detailed

knowledge of the market than any other factor (except perhaps your outsider help plan, discussed below). The market potential can be huge. There are over 100 countries to choose from, although only a few may be appropriate. You need a plan to get solid facts. You will want to minimize assumptions where error could be disaster. The three most important items to be checked are: 1) customer identity and opinions, 2) competitor strengths and weaknesses versus yours, and 3) mechanics such as distributors, personal visits, banks, money handling, regulations, tariffs, problems and extra costs, and taxes and other fees.

Here's how it might look.

Element to check	Data found
Our product and price	Management books. $39, retail.
Customer # and location	East Germany. Est 1.3 million.
Customer wants/trends	Big need for management guide. Big growth.
Competitor product	Few now. More soon. Samples available.
Competitor strengths	Good quality. Knows exporting.
Weaknesses (product, etc.)	Products not tuned, used for U.S.
Competitor price and packaging	Price too high. Package good.
Competitor personal distribution	No personal selling. No distributor.
Competitor publicity, ads	None, yet. Some, eventually. 2 years.
Our SWOT strengths	Better info, package, price, distributor.
Our weaknesses	More customer and distributor opinions.
Our opportunities	Growth market. Leads to others. ROI.
Mechanics, distribution, etc.	Personal trip soon to find good distributor.
Bank and forwarder	Freight forwarder has good bank help.
Red tape, tariffs, etc.	Freight forwarder knows all this.
Problems, insure, shipping	Program to be planned with distributor.

3. *Goal sheet*. Export goals and objectives should be reasonable and reachable. These would be for sales, profit, distribution level, ROI, awareness of the product, image and possibly for stock share sales by a certain point in time. Goals might be revised quarterly or annually as circumstances change.

Your goals might look something like the table below.

Goal element	1st Period	2nd Period	3rd Period
Sales (in thousands)	$50	$100	$250
Distributor level (retail)	5%	10%	25%
Profit (net)	(50)	(10)	50
ROI	Loss	Loss	20%
Awareness of product	2%	10%	20%
Stock shares sold (in thousands)	1	5	10

4. *Export testing plan*. This can be especially important in exporting, since the company is moving into an uncharted and unfamiliar market and venture. Many firms that fail to do their homework lose their shirts on export deals. They underestimate the complexity. Small tests are a low price to pay for avoiding this. Your export concept should be tested. Does it fit company structure, budget, prospect needs, and marketing ability? Then prospective export users should be checked to see if the sample product fits their needs or requires changes. Finally, before a major investment is made, the export market should be tested in a small area, a marketing program planned, executed, results measured, and needed changes made to be sure the program is profitable.

Here is a typical, successful set of export tests. Management judgment frequently need changes, but these adjustments usually result in good progress.

Test Plan Elements	Results Obtained
Concept fits company staff	Only slightly. Need training.
Concept fits company budget	A little. Must be modest plan.
Prospects liked concept	Yes. Foreign surveys said "Go!"
Sample liked use test	Yes, much. Small changes asked.
Use changes made, rechecked	Prospects said, "excellent."
Test market planned, made	Lasted 3 months, in 3 towns.
Test market results	Good. Advertising changes needed.
Recheck test market	Excellent. Sales above forecast.

5. *Marketing plan.* A marketing plan now becomes fairly easy. The tests have helped to design the right 8 P's (product, package, price, premium, promotion, personal selling, physical distribution and publicy/advertising). The guesswork and the risk has now been almost eliminated. (They are never totally removed, of course.) Here is a brief marketing plan example designed for exporting, using the 5 Ws, SWOT and 8 Ps:

Market Plan Elements	Information entered
Who	The Management Press.
What	Management book series.
When	1991 and 1992.
Where	Germany, later Poland, Hungary.
Why	To see increased sales, profits, ROI.
SWOT situation	New major markets opening for export.
Weapons	Good books ready. More soon.
Objectives	$50,000 year 1. $100,000 year 2.
Tactics/strategy: Products	Initially present line, then design.

Price	$39 at retail. $20 at distributor.
Package	Special reusable boxes.
Premiums	Display-rack with each dozen, retail.
Promotions	Coupon good for $1 off on next purchase.
Personal selling	By distributor rep to retailers.
Physical distribution	Through shipping points to retailers.
Publicity, ads	Mailers to retailers. Window banners.

6. Your export production plan should be carefully keyed to the marketing plan, so product type and volume is available just when needed and not much before. The plan should allow for lead time to cover shipping (by boat) and slower distribution in Europe than in U.S. Plan units produced by date, by volume, and by type of product. Also schedule various steps for each product. Start with only one or two products; expand as market patterns indicate. Consider initial production by local sources or nearby countries, since transport is a large part of total costs on heavy items.

Here's a brief example:

EXPORT PRODUCTION PLAN
by date, volume and product (in thousands)

Product	Jan	Feb	Mar	Apr	May	June	July	Aug
A	—	—	5	—	10	—	5	10
B	—	—	—	5	—	10	—	5
C	—	—	—	—	5	—	10	—

PRODUCTION STEPS

by period, people and product (A)

Steps	Per. 1	Per. 2	Per. 3	Per. 4
Design survey/test	xxx	—	—	—
Lab test/use test	—	xxx	—	—
Specs/equip ordered	—	—	xxx	—
Equip installed/tested	—	—	—	xxx
Supplies arrive, store	—	—	—	xxx
Product run/inventory	—	—	—	xxx
Product sold/shipped	—	—	—	—

The xxx's might be names of people taking action.

7. *Your finance plan* primarily should be your profit-and-loss forecast for several time periods. Since this shows losses and profits, it also amounts to a cash flow chart. It shows money in and money out. When cumulative figures are added, it also shows when total investment or cash flow into the venture equals cash out from the venture. At that point, it breaks even, so the chart also becomes a pay-out plan. Clearly, this is a handy, three-way record of profit-and-loss, cash flow, and the break-even point for your financial forecasting, strategic planning, and ongoing future control.

   Here is a simplified example:

Sales/Costs/Profit (in thousands)

	Per. 1	Per. 2	Per. 3	Per. 4
Sales income, this period	$50	$100	$250	$350
Cumulative	50	150	400	750
Costs, all, this period	150	100	200	200
Cumulative	150	250	450	650
Profit/loss, this period	(100)	0	50	150
Cumulative	(100)	(50)	0	100

8. Your export "people plan" begins with an inventory of skills to see what you have and what you need for an export program. The chances are that you have no professional export individual. But you may have a person who, on a part-time basis, could learn and help with the program. You should match people to the plan outlined so far. Show who does what and when. Prepare simple job specifications and a job description with a training schedule.

Here's a brief demonstration:

Duties	Who Does What	When
Company analysis	President and part-time export ex.	Per. 1
Industry fact plan	Pt. time exp. ex. + local rep.	Per. 1
Setting objectives	Pres, mkt exec., pt. timer	Per. 2
Testing plan	Pt. timer, local rep, mkt exec	Per. 2
Market plan	Pt. timer, local rep, mkt exec	Per. 3
Production plan	Pt. timer, production, & mkt exec	Per. 3
Finance plan	Pres, treasurer, pt. timer	Per. 3
People plan	Pres., pt timer, all officers	Per. 4
Outsider plan	Pres., pt timer, all officers	Per. 4
General strategic plan	Pres., pt timer, all officers	All

A personal visit to the foreign country can be one of the more interesting and exciting parts of the program. This should be done by the president or key marketing person. Objectives: to get an on-site feel, to see retail or other outlets, and most important, to arrange for a distributor. Letters and phone calls should be exchanged before the visit. A good itinerary should be set up. Good distributor prospects should be selected (perhaps two or three). In most foreign markets, the distributor relationship is a very personal one, and mutual trust (even dedication) between quality people is important. Exchange resumes, photo of the plant and staff, and details of the product. Allow much time for socializing. On arrival, have a checklist of information to get and to give. Take the candidate to visit some accounts and note the reception. Get a local contact to check the distributor references. Be friends, but be careful.

9. *Outside advisor help plan.* These resources are essential. Few initial exporters can go it alone. There are about a dozen good sources to check. The most important, by far, is usually the U.S. Department of Commerce. Its number one priority is to help companies export. They can provide you with three essentials: 1) market and prospect information (where to sell); 2) advice on simplifying your procedure (basic do's and don'ts, forms to fill out, tariffs, insurance, shipping, banks, how to bill and get paid, and other key points; 3) additional useful contacts. Most of this is free or low cost. The other sources of help and advice have been listed in a previous chapter; many will be able to assist your exporting efforts.

10. *Strategy by departments.* General export strategy normally requires part-time action from all groups. Exporting is rarely a full-time activity in small or mid-sized firms. Further, any export start-up situation facing a company is usually more complex, more delicate, more remote, more time consuming, and in need of more coordination than domestic programs. So you have *less* time available to handle a *more* complex project. This calls for extra care in strategic action. A schedule should be worked out, bringing all department skills together in synchronization.

DEMONSTRATION OF GENERAL EXPORT STRATEGY BY DEPARTMENTS

Department	Strategic Export Action (Start-up)
Production	Search for most efficient production methods. Check foreign regs. Foreign production source.
Sales	Detailed check of market, prospects and competition. Build top-quality distribution and incentives.
Finance	Check on all cash flow needs, solicit funds, make plans, check foreign exchange systems.
General Management	Plan and coordinate. Build production and mktg efficiency, outdo competitors, control costs.
Tech Dept	R & D work to exceed current competitors, and to fill customer needs better and cheaper.
Staff	Understand and support export effort. Learn new systems and markets. Provide superior service.

EXPORT ANALYSIS

Company situation	Favorable to export	Unfavorable
Profit level and trand		
Exportable product		
Strengths		
Ever exported		
Staff skills, exporting		
Staff time, exporting		
Advisors available		
Exporters known		

EXPORT ANALYSIS

INDUSTRY FACTS   Data Found

Our product and price

Customer number and location

Customer wants/trends

Competitor's product

Competitor's strengths

Weaknesses (product, etc.)

Competitor price & package

Competitor personal distribution

Competitor publicity, ads

Our SWOT strengths

Our weaknesses

Our opportunities

Mechanics, distribution, etc.

Bank and forwarder

Red tape, tariff, etc.

Problems, insur, ship

Remarks _____.

EXPORT ANALYSIS

Goal	1st Per.	2nd Per.	3rd Per.
Sales (in thousands)	$_____	$_____	$_____
Distribution level (retail)	_____%	_____%	_____%
Profit (net) [in thousands]	$_____	$_____	$_____
ROI	_____%	_____%	_____%
Awareness of product	_____%	_____%	_____%
Stock shares sold (in thousands)	_____	_____	_____

Remarks _____.

EXPORT ANALYSIS

Testing Plan	Results Obtained
Concept fits company staff	_____
Concept fits company budget	_____
Prospects like concept	_____
Sample liked use test	_____
Use changes made, rechecked	_____
Test market planned, made	_____
Test market results measured	_____
Test market recheck	_____

Remarks _____.

EXPORT ANALYSIS

Marketing Plan	Information Entered
Who	_____
What	_____
When	_____
Where	_____
Why	_____
SWOT situation	_____
Weapons	_____
Objectives	_____
Tactics/strategy	_____
Products	_____
Price	_____
Package	_____
Premiums	_____
Promotions	_____
Personal selling	_____
Physical distribution	_____
Publicity, ads	_____

Remarks _____.

EXPORT ANALYSIS

Production Volume by date and product (in thousands)

Product	J	F	M	A	M	J	J	A	S	O	N	D	Total
A	__	__	__	__	__	__	__	__	__	__	__	__	____
B	__	__	__	__	__	__	__	__	__	__	__	__	____
C	__	__	__	__	__	__	__	__	__	__	__	__	____

Productions Steps by period and product (A)

Steps	Per. 1	Per. 2	Per. 3	Per. 4	Per. 5
Design survey/test	____	____	____	____	____
Lab test/use test	____	____	____	____	____
Specs/equip ordered	____	____	____	____	____
Equip. installed/tested	____	____	____	____	____
Supplies arrive, store	____	____	____	____	____
Product run/inventory	____	____	____	____	____
Product sold/shipped	____	____	____	____	____

EXPORT ANALYSIS

Financial Plan

Sales/Costs/Profit (in thousands)	Per. 1	Per. 2	Per. 3	Per. 4
Sales income, this period	____	____	____	____
Cumulative	____	____	____	____
Costs total this period	____	____	____	____
Cumulative	____	____	____	____
Profit/loss this period	____	____	____	____
Cumulative	____	____	____	____

EXPORT ANALYSIS

People Plan	Who Does What	When
Company analysis plan	_____	_____
Industry fact plan	_____	_____
Setting objectives	_____	_____
Testing plan	_____	_____
Marketing plan	_____	_____
Production plan	_____	_____
Finance plan	_____	_____
People plan	_____	_____
Outsider plan	_____	_____
General strategy plan	_____	_____

EXPORT ANALYSIS

Outsider Help Plan

Help Source	Strategic Action Planned
Accountant	
Lawyer	
Dept of Commerce	
Exporter	
Forwarder	
Trade association	
Suppliers	
EXIM bank	
State Department	
Our local bank	
Dunn & Bradstreet	
SBA finance	
SBA/SCORE	
SBA/SBI	
SBA/SBDC	
Seminar	
Library	
Bookstore	

EXPORT ANALYSIS

General Stategy

Department	Strategic Export Action (Start-up)
Production	_____
Sales	_____
Finance	_____
General management	_____
Technical dept.	_____
Staff	_____

Follow these steps. Use these forms. Expand or reduce them as you adjust to your own situation, and you will greatly increase your chances of success in exporting.

17

Holding A Planning Session:

Victory By Design

A good leader is often nothing more than an ordinary person with extraordinary determination.
— Cervantes

The objective of this section is to give you a system for running a good planning meeting—one that gets good results, fast (with minimum effort on your part and maximum use of your staff's skills). Such a plan also generates a high level of personal involvement, commitment, and motivation, because you manage your resources well.

We will explain and demonstrate how to: select participants; set an agenda; state a mission; provide a useful premeeting form; arrange logistics; set a schedule; outline ground rules; go through the agenda points; and close so that constructive things happen.

How to select participants. These should be people who supervise each element of the business covered by your plan. This means people who organize, gather facts, test ideas or products, finance, produce, market, contact and work with outside people. Attendees should be people who know their area, have constructive suggestions, and can integrate or mesh their special operations with others in the company. Of course, one person may and often does handle several departments. A good planning group is usually three to thirty people, with six being ideal. Don't invite chair-warmers or nonparticipants. They simply clog up the works and interfere with progress. For our purposes, let's assume attendance by about six people out of a company of perhaps fifty employees.

How to prepare an agenda. At the top of the agenda, show title, date, time, place, who's attending, and meeting objective. Assuming the purpose is "to prepare a company plan," involving all parts of the business (and that this is rarely or never done), you might allow a full day. Perhaps a half hour or more for each element (like facts, tests, goals, budget, production, and marketing). Show subject, time, and person responsible for it. Allow time for a mid-morning and mid-afternoon break. You might have sandwiches brought in for lunch. This is a hard working meeting, not a social one. (But you may wish to allow for a social hour at the end.)

A short invitation note might be on the other side of the agenda page. This should contain a clear statement of the mission or purpose for the meeting. For example: "Our purpose is to review our problems and opportunities, set goals and suggest ways to meet them." Briefly indicate rules for the meeting such as, "All ideas are welcome." "Hold criticism until we get to the decision stage." "When we finish the meeting we want to have mutually agreed upon some firm plans." Send this to participants a week or two before the meeting.

Provide a blank planning form to each attendee. You will find suggested forms in each section of this volume. For example, there are forms for fact gathering, production, marketing, and so on. That will allow attendees to do a lot of thinking before the meeting. Ideas will be more constructive.

Organize your logistics and mechanics. Failure here can ruin a meeting. Excellent facilities can sometimes make a session. Be sure the location is convenient, with enough parking, a good meeting room, chairs, table, heat, air conditioning, rest rooms, coffee or soft drinks, ash trays, flip charts (blank or with material), paper, pens, and folders.

Begin with a recap of the purpose for the meeting. Then offer a review of general procedure, agenda, and plans form items. Then go right to the SWOT formula and start with the situation, both in the company and outside of it. Proceed to cover weapon resources, opportunities, and threats or problems. Let each person make a brief statement, if practical. Take some notes. Get some goal ideas from the group by again going around the room.

Try brainstorming when you get to tactics or strategy ideas for reaching goals. Here, anything goes. There are no wrong answers. Ideas can be freewheeling, wild, off the wall. Write them down. Reality can set in later. But sometimes goofy ideas, modified, lead to constructive strategies.

Cover the basic planning formulas of 5 Ws, SWOT, 8 P's and KRA's. These mean: who, what, when, where, why; situation, weapon resources, opportunities, tactics/strategy; product, package, price, premium, promotion, physical distribution, personal selling, publicity and advertising; and Key Result Areas (such as profits).

Now *firm up plans*, select the best of your options and suggestions and ideas. Get general, all-around agreement. Write these down for future use. Summarize, state conclusions, and outline the next three steps. Who does what, when, and where.

Follow up the meeting with a written one- or two-page summary. In the cold light of dawn, people may have second thoughts (or better thoughts). Perhaps prepare your plans document draft as the follow-up. Distribute it to attendees and perhaps other interested parties.

Here is a demonstration of a plans meeting blueprint.

Participants	Head of marketing, production, finance, technicians
Agenda	5 W's, time slots, key person, lunch.
Invitation	Purpose, ground rules.
Blank form	Form for each department and total company plans form.
Logistics	Hilton Hotel, good meeting room, arranged.
Beginning	Our goal today, rules, situation, weapons
Brainstorm	Anything. No wrong ideas. Lets dream!

Formulas	<u>5W's, SWOT, 8 P's, KRA's.</u>
Firm-up plans	<u>Last 3 hours. 30 minutes/department</u>
Note-taking	<u>Secretary will note key points. Not all.</u>
Summary	<u>Each person gives 1-minute summary, his area.</u>
Follow-up	<u>We'll draft a plan from notes and summaries.</u>

PLANNING SESSION FORM

Participants	_____
Agenda	_____
Invitation	_____
Blank form	_____
Logistics	_____
Beginning	_____
Brainstorm	_____
Formulas	_____
Firm-up plans	_____
Note-taking	_____
Summary	_____
Follow-up	_____

Follow this meeting plan and you will develop a corporate program that will be more profitable. Your plans will be superior to those of your competitors. Your program will increase productivity, morale, and motivation. This is victory by design. Enjoy it!

Part III

Countdown to a Successful Plan

18

Why Plans Fail—and How to Avoid This

The power of positive thinking is great to behold.

—N. V. Peal

The purpose of this section is to look at weak spots, the points where you and I are most likely to fail. To be forewarned is to be forearmed!

Learn from the mistakes of others. This increases your efficiency. Let them take the hits; you take the knowledge. When you do a little of this homework and do it seriously, you improve your position if and when you are tested with challenges. Suddenly big problems become little ones. And your cost is far lower than the price of failure.

This is not to say that we will or should dwell on the negatives. But problems are worth at least a look. Good doctors, lawyers, pilots, architects, investors, and managers learn a lot about preventive maintenance by studyings diseases, errors, and disorders.

We will see some common causes of planning failure: no plan at all, halfway commitment, overdone, overengineered, or overly complex, automatic, ambitious, rigid, or precise plans. Let's look at each.

1. No plan simply means either no awareness of or just no consideration of the planning process (or of the advantages to it). Or it may mean simply a lack of a key part. For examples, no facts, no SWOT, no clear, goals or no strategy program. Management purely by feel, intuition, from day to day without any forward plans, by reaction, or even management by crisis. It works sometimes, but not often.

   Any great business, shopping mall, college, cultural or entertainment center, government program, publisher, banker, utility, or hospital used planning (a lot of planning). Small firms who grew bigger did the same thing.

2. A halfway commitment can be expensive. Steps are taken, investing time, money, and effort. What follows? Poor communication, with negative effects on delegation, team acceptance, management support, budgets or schedules. Often, a planner is assigned who has no credibility, stature, prestige, or clout. No monitoring, no mid-course corrections, no results. Failure to follow through is another problem. Often a fully developed plan is completed, circulated, adjusted, admired, and then filed away without any further action. Perhaps it was done simply as something to do, or for some group, such as the board of directors. But it eventually becomes a bad joke that discredits company management.

3. The over-engineered or overly complex program is perhaps the most costly error of all. American managers have a habit of going from one extreme to another. Either no planning is done or far too much. Here a large dollar investment is made, often too large. ("If one is good, then ten must be better!") A great deal of time is spent. Hundreds of pages are written and charts completed.

   This sometimes becomes so complex that nobody understands the plan. The program gets hopelessly gridlocked. It becomes too big, too expensive, and more trouble than it's worth. Not much happens (but a lot of money is spent). Managers become disillusioned, then angry, and soon start looking for someone to blame. Often the planner or plans assistant or trainee is sent packing. Planning becomes a dirty word. In truth, the error was not the *idea*, but the *method*.

4. Often a mistaken belief creeps in, that a highly developed, mechanical method is somehow so brilliant that it will operate all by itself. We Americans are fascinated by gadgets, gimmicks, machines and mechanics. "If a microwave oven can operate by itself, why can't a planning process do the same?" However, even with machinery or an advanced computer, someone must program it, start it, feed it, monitor progress, adjust it, measure results, and so forth, not to mention turn it off at night.

5. Overly ambitious, unrealistic goals often suffer the tragedy of excessive expectations. No matter what limited good results come out of the plan, these are never enough, and always seem a disappointment compared to goals. Result: money is invested, progress is made. But management is not pleased and is not likely to use the planning process again. Once more, plans becomes a dirty word: "We tried it once before and it didn't work." The problem, again, was not the planning but the method.

6. Plans that are too rigid often fail. Plans should be short, simple, understandable, practical, and workable. They should allow management to speed up or slow down or change direction and make new plans quickly as new market situations or opportunities or products appear. Says Peter Drucker, "Don't let management tools become management masters." The plan is there to serve you; you are not there to serve it. Use it as a tool. Change it when it's necessary.

7. Another frequent error is expecting all parts of the program to work out *exactly* as anticipated. They seldom do. Few wars, business ventures, or poker games come out exactly as planned. Accept this and work for the best plan you can nevertheless.

Sometimes people don't reach goals. Other times they exceed them. And sometimes they simply get results that are different from expectations, opening new doors and new vistas. Wise managers take advantage of these. But without the plan, nothing much *at all* would have happened.

A SYSTEM FOR AVOIDING ERRORS

Errors We'll Avoid	Steps We'll Take at A.B.C. Company
Low commitment	We'll put in enough to do the job.
Incomplete plan	We'll use forms and checklists.
Low communications	We'll be sure all understand and buy it.
Low delegation	We'll make specific assignments.
Low team acceptance	Be sure team is a part and supports.
Poor schedule	We'll make the time frame realistic.
Low planner status	Be sure planner has credibility.
Low monitoring	Monitor often. Especially at first.
Low follow-through	If we plan it, we do it!
Low adjustment	Adjustment as needed. It's not frozen.
Low results	Be sure enough good happens.
Too complex	Keep it simple, so easily followed.
Expect automation	We'll be sure people are involved.
Overly ambitious	Be sure goals and strategy are realistic.
Too rigid	Stay flexible (adjust to conditions).
Too precise	We'll accept various good results.

ERROR-KILLER CHECKLIST

Errors	Steps Taken to Avoid Error
Low commitment	
Incomplete plan	
Low communications	
Low delegation	
Low team acceptance	
Poor schedule	
Low planner status	
Low monitoring	
Low follow-through	
Low adjustment	
Low results	
Too complex	
Expect automation	
Overly ambitious	
Too rigid	
Too precise	

If you can avoid these errors, then you have an excellent chance of building a fine plan and making it work. Your employees, owners and competitors will have new respect for you and your company. And they will also respect your new profits.

19

Problems Solved:

How To Snatch Victory From Defeat

They attack, we retreat. They stop, we stop. They sleep, we attack.
— Mao

Lead, follow, or get out of the way.
— Ted Turner

Let's face it, stuff happens. Errors, problems, and new situations occur. The most common challenges are, first, errors are made in the plan itself. Second, even the best laid plans almost never happen exactly as expected. They often take more time, money, and effort than anticipated. And third, almost every week or every day, new conditions arise.

These call for mid-course corrections. The wise planner anticipates new problems and knows how to solve them, or, better still, prevents them from occurring in the first place. Prevention is usually far more efficient than correction.

Our purpose here is to anticipate problems and prevent them, primarily by taking positive steps to see that difficulties don't bite us in the back when we least expect them.

The best preventative actions include good communication and involvement of key people, with proper investment, checking, flexibility, adjustment, and testing—all focusing on realistic results.

1. *Communicate.* Be sure all leaders understand the plans, the situation, objectives, tactics, their role and the roles of others, the investment and the expected results. Good communication avoids a multitude of difficulties.

2. *Get involvement.* Be sure everyone is a part of the program. Get them to consider it not as the plan, but our plan. This will prevent problems because, instead of saying, "I see where your plan has hit a snag," they will say, "Our plan ran into a little difficulty, and I fixed it!"

3. *Keep involved.* Check back with them frequently, especially during the early stages. Get their ideas. Use their suggestions whereever possible. Keep 'em sold.

4. *Focus on key people*—leaders. With their support, problems will be avoided or quickly solved.

5. *Proportion your investment* of time and effort for both the plan and its execution. Avoid over- or under-investment. These are major causes of problems. Put in just enough to do the job properly.

6. *Get playback.* Watch every step. Imagine problems and take steps to prevent them from happening. Remember Murphy's law: "Anything that can go wrong, will go wrong." Arrange so it almost can't happen. Think along the lines of driving: move where they can't hit you.

7. *Stay flexible.* Be ready to slow down, speed up, change direction, take advantage of opportunities, or fix things if the situation indicates.

   German physicians have a saying, "The best doctors are not necessarily those who always make the right diagnosis—but who recognize any error, and correct it immediately." Be especially alert to new surprise markets or new products or services that open profit possibilities. Keep an open mind. Nothing should be cast in concrete. Be ready, willing and able to take new directions — or even to make a totally new plan. And do this quickly. That way, a threat, challenge, or problem quickly converts to an opportunity for income.

8. *Respond to tests.* When these cry "TILT!" be sure your group has the discipline and patience to stop and fix what needs fixing. When tests say "GO!" have the confidence to do just that. When they say "GOOD RESULTS," communicate and spread the good news to all involved.

9. *Focus on good results* from every group. Get a regular measure of actual progress versus planned goals. Be more concerned with *what* happens than *how* it happens (as long as it is within budget, legal, and in good taste). Some managers waste time by being less concerned with results than with whether people did it like they were told.

10. *Stay lean, mean, simple, and practical* (not cushy, casual, complex, or dreamy).

11. *Trust common sense.* Make reasonable, affordable investments of time, money, and effort in planning and executing the program; and expect reasonable results.

A PROBLEM PREVENTION PLAN

Tactical Steps	How We Plan to Do It
Communicate	Meet. Discuss. Agree. Use forms. Review.
Get involvement	Make it our plan. No edicts or orders.
Keep involvement	Get their ideas. Use these. Keep selling.
Key people	Identify leaders. Show support profits.
Proportion investment	Put in enough, but don't overdo.
Get playback	Watch action. Spot potential trouble.
Stay flexible	Adjust to new situations and opportunity.
Respond to tests	If no, stop. If go, go. Inform all.
Focus on results	Measure outcome and income.
Stay practical	Avoid overly casual or overly complex plans.
Common sense	Expect reasonable investments and results.

PROBLEM PREVENTION FORM

Tactical Steps	How We Plan to Do It
Communicate	_____
Get involvement	_____
Keep involvement	_____
Key people	_____
Proportion invest	_____
Get playback	_____
Stay flexible	_____
Respond to tests	_____
Focus on results	_____
Stay practical	_____
Common sense	_____

Use this simple form, and you will avoid over ninety percent of the problems that hit planners. Your planning will be realistic, effective, fairly troublefree, and generate enthusiastic progress.

20

Strategic Plans Form

Success often comes from not repeating the same mistake.
— Henderson

The outline provided here gives you a number of advantages.

First it can be used pretty much as it is, to become your plan.

Second you can use it as a summary or overview, then attach extra pages for the parts you want to expand, such as marketing or finance.

Third it puts things in perspective, showing the broad spectrum of activities. It slows down any wildly enthusiastic action just long enough to ask some cold, hard questions.

Fourth it is thorough, serving as a good checklist that may spark new thoughts.

Fifth it provides you with safeguards, such as market research and people plans to help prevent failure.

Sixth it is a good training device for the new planner or assistant.

Seventh perhaps best of all, over recent years it has provided progress and profits in hundreds of firms in the U.S. and around the world.

In the end, it becomes an almost automatic method that lets you do above-average planning at below-average costs and investments of time.

It repeats and shortens some items, such as the executive summary and the main plan. Some people only have time to read the summary, while scanning the rest. Also, to provide you with a condensed, consolidated package, this Seven-Part Plan picks up and shortens forms from preceding sections. Where more detail is wanted, those longer forms can replace the shorter ones used here.

Items are also repeated in much shorter versions in the next section, should you need to do a plan in a very small amount of time.

CONDENSED STRATEGIC PLAN

1. EXECUTIVE SUMMARY PAGE

Company: _____

Address: _____ Phone: _____

Title of the plan: _____

Prepared by: _____

Addressed to: _____

The Basic Idea: _____

_____

SWOT Summary

The primary or key
Situation is: _____

Weapon resource is: _____

Objective is: _____

Tactic is: _____

Remarks: _____

Feasibility Tests

Why will this plan succeed? _____

What do tests show (concept, use, market)? _____

Key benefit to our company: _____

Remarks: _____

Tactics Summary (Mark-Prod-Fin POST)

Market Plan: _____

Product Plan: _____

Finance Plan: _____

People Plan: _____

Outsider Plan: _____

Sell the Plan: _____

Time of Plan: _____

Remarks: _____

2. SITUATION: MARKET FACTS

5 W's Currently in the Market

What are we selling? _____

Who are our best prospects? _____

Where are they? _____

Why will they buy? _____

Who are our competitors? _____

Why are we better? _____

What needs do we fill? _____

What wants do we fill? _____

What is the market size? _____

What are market trends? _____

What do prospects like? _____

What do prospects dislike? _____

Do prospects like Our idea? _____ SAMPLE _____

Where do they buy? _____ When? _____

What is our sales forecast? _____

Remarks: _____

What are our 8 P's currently?

Product _____ Package _____

Price _____ Premium _____

Promotion _____ Person Sell _____

Physical Distribution _____ Publicity _____

Remarks: _____

Our Situation SWOT Currently

Strengths: _____

Weaknesses: _____

Opportunities: _____

Threats: _____

Remarks: _____

3. WEAPON RESOURCES (Company Facts)

Who are our key managers? _____

What is our business? _____

What are our key departments? _____

Why did we grow? _____

What are our strengths? _____

Weaknesses? _____

Opportunities? _____

Threats? _____

Best resources? _____

Remarks? _____

4. OUR OBJECTIVES (in thousands)

	Year #1	Year #2	Remarks
Sales	$ _____	$ _____	_____
Costs	$ _____	$ _____	_____
Profits	$ _____	$ _____	_____
Market share	_____ %	_____ %	_____
Awareness/image	_____	_____	_____
Sales of stock	_____	_____	_____
Staff size	_____	_____	_____
New products/services	_____	_____	_____

Is our goal mainly to survive? _____

To grow? _____

Remarks: _____

5. MARKET PLAN

SITUATION (Market) (Summary of plan 2, carried forward)

Who will buy? _____

What will they buy? When? _____

Where? Why? _____

Remarks: _____

WEAPON RESOURCES (Ours) (Summary of plan 3, carried forward)

Strengths: _____

Weaknesses: _____

Opportunities: _____

Threats: _____

Remarks: _____

MARKET OBJECTIVES (Summary of plan 4, carried forward)

	Year #1	Year #2	Remarks
Sales	$ _____	$ _____	_____
Awareness	_____%	_____%	_____
Image	_____	_____	_____
Net distribution	_____%	_____%	_____
Market share	_____%	_____%	_____

Remarks _____

MARKET TACTICS (New plans, near future)

Product _____ Package _____

Price _____ Premium _____

Promotion _____ Person Selling _____

Physical Distribution _____ Publicity _____

Advertising theme _____

Advertising media (key) _____

Remarks _____

MARKET TIME Schedule (for key marketing steps)

Who: _____ Does what: _____

When: _____ Where: _____ Why: _____

Remarks _____

6. PRODUCTION PLAN

Schedule	J	F	M	A	M	J	J	A	S	O	N	D
Product A	__	__	__	__	__	__	__	__	__	__	__	__
Product B	__	__	__	__	__	__	__	__	__	__	__	__
Product C	__	__	__	__	__	__	__	__	__	__	__	__

Remarks: _____

Production steps by period, people and product

Steps	Per. 1	Per. 2	Per. 3	Per. 4	Per. 5
Design survey/test	____	____	____	____	____
Lab test/use test	____	____	____	____	____
Specifications/ equipment ordered	____	____	____	____	____
Supplies arrive/store	____	____	____	____	____
Product run/inventoried	____	____	____	____	____
Product sold/shipped	____	____	____	____	____

Remarks: _____

7. FINANCE PLAN (Cash flow)

Sales/Cost/Profit (thousands)	Per. 1	Per. 2	Per. 3	Per. 4
Sales income, this period	$ ____	$ ____	$ ____	$ ____
Cumulative	$ ____	$ ____	$ ____	$ ____
Costs, all, this period	$ ____	$ ____	$ ____	$ ____
Cumulative	$ ____	$ ____	$ ____	$ ____
Profit (loss) this period	$ ____	$ ____	$ ____	$ ____
Cumulative	$ ____	$ ____	$ ____	$ ____

Remarks: _____

8. PEOPLE PLAN

	Who Does What	When
Candidate specifications	_____	_____
Position descriptions	_____	_____
Job training	_____	_____
Personnel skills inventory	_____	_____
Organization plan	_____	_____
Expansion plan	_____	_____
Recruiting sources	_____	_____
Compensation statement	_____	_____
Motivation program	_____	_____
Planning leaders	_____	_____
Personnel records	_____	_____

Remarks: _____

9. OUTSIDER PLAN

Action expected from

Accountant _____	Service clubs _____
Our Lawyer _____	Realtor _____
Our Banker _____	Management Consultant _____
Suppliers _____	SBA _____
Business friends _____	SBI _____
Technicians _____	SCORE _____
Advertising Agency _____	SBDC _____
Local Chamber _____	Seminars/Books _____
Tax Service _____	Public Relations Agency _____
Trade Associations _____	Export Sources _____

Remarks (others) _____

10. SELLING THE PLAN

Here's how we'll do each step:

Preparation _____	Tone _____
Explain program _____	Questions _____
Show user values _____	Answers _____
Give out plan _____	Humor _____
Stay simple _____	Get to "Yes" _____
Push teamwork _____	Plan summary _____
Focus on results _____	Delegate jobs _____
Use visuals _____	Close up-beat _____
Practice _____	Ask for OK _____

Remarks: _____

11. TIME PLAN

Next 3 Steps

Person	Action	Due Date
1._____	_____	_____
2._____	_____	_____
3._____	_____	_____

Remarks _____

12. FEEDBACK and Adjustments

Who gets feedback? _____

What data is sought? _____

Why? _____

When is this due? _____

Where does this come from? _____

Who reviews it? _____

What is done with this? _____

Remarks: _____

Plan prepared by: _____ (date)_____

Plan approved by: _____ (date)_____

21

High-Speed Short Form:
The 10-Minute Plan

Management is the ability to get things done through others.
— Kettering

Herewith the "bare bones" version of the information in the previous chapter. Use these materials when a "quickie" approach is appropriate: i.e., for those requiring only a thumbnail sketch of your plan.

Title: _____ Date: _____

Company name: _____

Basic idea: _____

_____

1. MARKET SITUATION (Feasibility)

Do prospects like our concept? _____

Do they like our sample/model? _____

Were there purchases in the test market? _____

Why will prospects buy? _____

Why are we better than competition? _____

_____

What need do we fill? _____

Remarks: _____

2. WEAPON RESOURCES (COMPANY FACTS)

Strengths: _____ Opportunities: _____

Weaknesses: _____ Threats: _____

Remarks: _____

3. OBJECTIVES

Objectives	Per. 1	Per. 2
Sales	$ _____	$ _____
Profits	$ _____	$ _____

Remarks: _____

4. MARKET PLAN

Product/Service _____ Promotion: _____

Packaging: _____ Person. Sell: _____

Price: _____ Physical distribution: _____

Premiums: _____ Public Relations: _____

Advertising: _____

Remarks: _____

5. PRODUCTION PLAN

Start date: _____ Volume: _____

Total cost: $ _____ Unit cost: $ _____

Remarks: _____

6. FINANCE PLAN

Amount needed $_____ Borrow $ _____

Cash on hand $ _____ Sell shares $ _____

Remarks: _____

7. PEOPLE PLAN

Staff needed: _____ Duties: _____

Sources: _____ Training: _____

Remarks: _____

8. OUTSIDER PLAN

Banker/lawyer: _____ Friends: _____

Accountant/supplier: _____ SBA: _____

Remarks: _____

9. SELLING THE PLAN

Prepare: _____ Give summary: _____

Show $ goals: _____ Ask for OK: _____

Remarks: _____

10. TIME PLAN (Next 3 steps)

Who Does What	When
1. _____	_____
2. _____	_____
3. _____	_____

Remarks _____

MAXWELL SMART'S
"THE OLD BACK-OF-THE-ENVELOPE PLAN"

Date: _____

Company: _____

SWOT: Situation, Weapon, Objective, Tactics

Situation (5 W's): _____

Inside: _____

Outside: _____

Weapon Resources: _____

_____

Objective: _____

Tactics: _____

Market (8 P's): _____

(Feasible?) _____

Product: _____

Finance (Sales) $ _____

(Profit) $ _____

People: _____

Outsiders: _____

Sell the idea: _____

Time (next step): _____

BACK-OF-A-BUSINESS-CARD PLAN

SWOT: Situation, Weapons, Objectives, Tactics

Tactics: Mark-Prod-Fin-POST

Market, Production, Finance,

People, Outsiders, Selling the idea, Time

22

Seven Successes You Can Imitate

Learn from the mistakes of others. You can't live long enough to make them all yourself.

— Vanbee

Here are seven real-life successful cases. The managers faced serious problems, used the SWOT planning formula, and achieved high levels of success.

This section will summarize these cases, each of which highlights a key planning point and how it was used. These examples may spark some practical application that you can use in your own business. Some suggestions are listed as well.

The seven cases will include three very small firms, two small ones, and two mid-sized ones. They are spread across the country, in a wide and fairly representative cross-section of American industries: service, manufacturing, retail, finance, publishing, medicine, and transportation.

This table shows the breakdown in more detail.

Tactic/Plan	Size*	Type	Company Name
1. Market Plan	very small	Service	N.Y. TV Productions
2. Product Plan	small	Manufacturer	Hand Soaps R Us
3. Finance Plan	mid-size	Retailer	S.W. Wood Supplies
4. People Plan	very small	Finance	Denver Mall National Bank
5. Outsider Plan	small	Publishing	American Institute of Management
6. Sell Plan	mid-size	Medicine	California State Hospital
7. Time Plan	very small	Transport	O'Hare Limousine Service

* very small is under 10 employees. Small is 10 to 50.

1. *Market Plan.* New York TV Productions is a group made up of two brothers and their wives, each with some experience in editing, tagging, playback, dubbing commercials and TV shows. They set up their own shop five years ago. Their problem was slow profit growth. Their solution was better marketing.

   Situation: A large and growing—but competitive—market.

   Weapon resources: Lots of experience, skills, contacts.

   Objectives: Raise gross from current $1.5 to $2.5 million.

   Tactics: Mainly "Marketing Plans" and execution. The group prepared a questionnaire about prospect needs and interviewed their contacts on a personal basis. They were surprised to find a lack of low-cost business management videotape facilities in part of their market. They offered just such a service to local firms, consultants, and business college people.

   Result: volume exceeded goal by a good measure, and a branch opened in Los Angeles.

Point you can use: Know market needs; set goals; take action.

2. *Produce Plan.* Hand Soaps R Us is a small manufacturer with years of experience in the cleaning compound business. Management wanted to expand into the higher-profit consumer hand soap field. They changed their name, but had difficulty developing a superior product.

Situation: Large, competitive market. No strong entry.

Weapon resources: Skills at formulating cleaning agents.

Objective: Get into larger market via better product.

Tactics: The company focused their business strategy on their Product Plan. Their technical people worked closely with their suppliers to develop an excellent, soft-soap, gooplike product. This was given a clever name and package, tested with users, and introduced into test markets.

Result: Major growth; expansion; large profit increase.

Point you can use: Recognize market needs and your product strengths available to fill those needs. Use range of talent.

3. *Finance Plan.* S.W. Wood Supply Shop is a mid-sized retail chain offering specialty tools and woods for the upscale carver. Growth had been steady and a strategic plan was prepared, focusing on a major financial program expansion. Their problem was that the managers were not quite sure how to do this.

Solution: They used financial schedules to plan and project.

Situation: Growth; ideas; financial program; no plan, yet.

Weapon resources: A good record of profits and ROI.

Objectives: To make a sound financial plan.

Tactics: Good formats were examined. At first these became so complex that people had trouble understanding them. Then they were streamlined and simplified into projections of costs, profit and loss, cash flow (breakeven, payout plan), and balance sheets.

Results: These were used. Some results were better than expected, others were not. But total was favorable.

Point you can use: If a good financial plan is needed, keep it realistic, simple, clear, and understandable.

4. *People Plan.* Denver Mall National Bank is a very small, independent savings and loan. Their problem was the recent negative publicity in their industry, which created a strong decline in deposits. The solution came from better use of their employees.

   Situation: Good market and service, but bad image.

   Weapon resources: Skilled people, plus desire to improve.

   Objective: Raise their community stature and deposits.

   Tactics: Management focused on their people plan, especially training; published and videotaped material on building better public relations were used, along with a skilled consultant.

   Results: Morale, status, and deposits went up sharply.

   Point you can use: Good people, well trained and motivated, can make a major difference in your bottom line.

5. *Outsider Plan.* American Institute of Management is a small, northwestern publisher of management material. Their problem was steady profit decline. Their solution was use of free SBA/SCORE/SBI/SBDC consultant services to improve their strategic planning.

   Situation: Poor trends on income and profits.

   Weapon resources: Aggressive management plus free resources.

   Objective: Turn the company around toward sales/profit growth.

   Tactics: Management prepared a strategic program with special emphasis on the outsider plan. These people came up with a number of new, affordable steps, new products, new markets, and new ways to reach them.

   Results: Sales and profits have steadily increased.

   Point you can use: Don't forget that there are lots of skilled outside resources (free or low cost) who can offer major help.

6. *Selling the Plan.* Central Cal State Hospital had developed a fine strategic plan, but there it sat, gathering dust on the shelf. These were medical people, not marketing people. No one knew how to sell it to the top state structure and

finance people. The solution was to generate and execute a specific selling plan for the program.

Situation: A good strategy plan, but no way to push it.

Weapon resource: Help available to improve presentation.

Objective: To achieve acceptance by top financial groups.

Tactics: The hospital managers focused on ways to sell their strategy plan. Their advertising agency helped them build a sound, effective selling program.

Result: The top authorities were highly impressed, and the strategy plan was enthusiastically accepted.

Point you can use: Don't expect a good plan to sell itself to lenders, investors, the public, employees or others. Design a program to be *sure* your plan is accepted.

7. *Time Plan.* O'Hare Limousine Service is a very small independent operator, serving special suburban customers. Their problem was excessive competition during peak hours. Their solution, evolving over several years, was one of better scheduling.

   Situation: Slow company growth, serious market competition.

   Weapon resources: Good service, creative management.

   Objective: To improve profits and overcome competition.

   Tactics: Management recognized that improved availability during peak times would make an important difference. Their strategic plan focused on their timing plan. They got detailed flight schedules, programmed their small desktop computer, and tied this into their radio communications.

   Results: Good planning focusing on time scheduling to improve service produced big profits.

   Point you can use: Occasionally, your time plan can give you important competitive advantages.

These cases give you an idea of how to apply the seven key tactics of a strategy plan: market plan, production plan, finance plan, people plan, outsider plan, selling the plan, and timing plan. Good planners focus on the one(s) most needed to maximize progress for their company and themselves.

23

Training a Planner Assistant

Give a man a fish and you feed him for a day. Teach him to fish and you feed him for a life.

—J. Harvard

Does this sound familiar?

"My problem is that my time is very limited. I don't have much chance for planning because there are so many other urgent priorities. You know how it is. Things must be done right now!" Solution: Train another person as a part-time planning assistant. Someone who is motivated, able, and credible.

The fastest way to train a planner is to explain, demonstrate, and let him practice doing it.

Six easy steps are to:

1. define the process,

2. screen and select a person for doing it,

3. orient the new person to the job duties,

4. review the system, let him sit in with a planning session and then try doing some small projects,

5. use careful observation, coaching, and supervision, and

6. provide adequate incentives and motivation.

This person can save a great deal of time for all of top management, invest enough hours to really do the job properly, and become truly proficient in a relatively short time. This will make him useful for other, similar projects in the future.

Keep in mind that total company plans are the realm of top management. Management can and should delegate as conditions permit. But even though someone else handles the mechanics—and does it well—management must still review, control, correct, and approve the final product. Top management knows things that few others possibly could. As Pete Drucker says, "Delegate, but don't abdicate!"

The best basic method is that used by top professional educators in law, medicine, architecture, finance and others: explanation, demonstration, and practical action.

ERRORS TO AVOID

Here are things that can damage or even destroy a plans program and hurt the company. First, lack of knowledge. Insufficient insight into the company or the plans system can be a real handicap. (This book can help with the system and guide data gathering about the company.) Second, what might be called the "too's": too many people expecting too much, too fast. Good plans training is rarely done over a cup of coffee. Third, not working well or close enough with other key members. Good plans training doesn't happen in a vacuum; it needs considerable communication. Fourth, underestimating the amount of preparation needed, the size of the job, or the effect it has on the organization. A fifth error is investing a lot of time in learning the planning system and then not using it.

The material you have in your hands is designed to help you avoid these problems.

Here are the six key steps to training a good planner and doing it fairly fast.

1. *Define just what you mean by planning.* Perhaps also include what you do not mean. Hardly any two top leaders define planning the same way, so that gives you a lot of latitude. If the leader has a tough time doing this, it will be even harder for the student. Make a reasonable commitment to the time needed for training, based on results expected.

   A part of your definition should be preparing a short job description for the planner. This can be a simple set of sentences outlining duties. Now the planner will know what is expected.

   You will find that this list of duties also serves you in another way. They help to clarify and even point to the specifications for a good candidate. For example, if one of the duties is gathering facts or writing a strategy plan, then one of the job specifications might be: "Experience collecting data or writing documents." Your specifications, at the very least, probably should be something like: "Candidate is a person who has some knowledge of the company and industry, plus a willingness to learn and ability to work with managers—and some interest in and experience with at least simple forward planning."

   One final specification you should seriously consider is a rather abstract, subjective quality that we might call credibility. This means someone who is respected by others, someone who, with training, would be at least partly accepted or given a chance to prove themselves as a planner. This should not be an entry-level person.

   Now you have a definition, list of duties, and personnel position specifications. All three can fit on one page.

   These probably add up to an inside, on-board person, rather than an outside person, although this is not always true. Past experience shows that ideal people are usually a partner, an executive vice president, a department head, an assistant, or an intelligent, experienced executive secretary.

2. *Screening and selection.* At this point, selection of available candidates becomes a lot easier for you because you have done preparation and homework. Now, you can simply match each candidate with the job specifications. You may not have many options, and by this time, the selection may be fairly obvious. The job is usually less than half time, often only a few weeks per year, at most, so this factor may influence your selection.

3. *Orienting the new planner trainee should be just a matter of covering a few key points.* First, your philosophy or way of looking at planning. Then the 5 W's. What it is, who does it, when, where and why. You might review both the job duties and the job specifications. Your trainee also will be interested in learning what support you expect to provide and where the planner fits in the organization. You might outline how the plans procedure will be followed, who helps, what will be done with the final plan, and how this is expected to help the company. (You and some of your colleagues might be interested in that same data.)

   An important part of this stage is orienting other key company people. Be sure they know about the training effort. Solicit their understanding, opinions, cooperation, and assistance. They are likely to give all of this freely if they see the planner as a friend, a time-saver, and a voice representing their interests

4. *EX-DEM-PRA stands for "Explanation, Demonstration, and Practical projects."* This is a handy formula used by some of the most successful professional educators. Explanation can simply mean elaboration or expansion of the orientation plus a more detailed review of the planning process. You will also want the trainee to review the total company information, market facts, and various department plans forms. The trainee should discuss these with department heads and change the format to fit your specific company.

   The demonstration might be to fill out a practice or sample version of these forms, just to get used to the idea and the system. (Or, if you have the time, the trainee might be invited to sit in and observe the entire planning process.)

The practical work is most effective if it is an actual role or part in a real planning procedure.

5. *Supervision, involving close coaching, especially in the early steps of the training process.* Eventually you can back away a bit and let the planner try preparing some short plans forms independently. Don't leave the trainee stranded, but, on the other hand, avoid oversupervising. Seek a middle ground, where the trainee feels free to touch base with the lead person as needed.

The next stage of supervision is to get playback from both the planner and the key department people. This may call for some mid-course corrections. At this point, if all is well, the planner assistant can begin to play a major role in the plans meetings. The planner assistant should be able to help with initial drafting, circulation for review, adjustment, final preparation and group presentation.

6. *Providing incentives adequate to generate strong motivation.* This might be the possibility of a bonus, salary increase, or promotion. Other things can work as well or even better than money, such as company stature and respect, recognition, awards, or even the feeling of accomplishing something worthwhile by improving company growth.

Here is a demonstration of this plans training program.

Step or Element	Action Our Company Will Take
Knowledge	Use company resources, this book and others.
Expectations	Reasonable results in reasonable time.
Work with others	Close work with all key people.
Preparation	Work volume and time needs are recognized.
Follow-through	Specific future steps are scheduled.
Planning defined	An orderly statement of company growth.
Time investment	About 20 hours/week, 4 weeks/year.
Job description	To know and help with total program.
Specification for planner	Knows the business, willing, credible.
Screening	We'll match candidates with specifications.
Orienting planner	Check job specifications, goal, role, results, 5 W's.
Orienting executives	Tell program, ask for opinions and help.
Explanation	Discuss forms and systems.
Demonstration	Fill in forms, then watch plans meetings.
Practical work	Draft part, route, discuss, change.
Coaching	Close at first, later less often.
Independence	Planner prepares material on own.
Touch base	Check with each other periodically.
Corrections	Adjustments as requested and needed.
Final action	Complete plan, submit, sell to groups.
Incentives	Financial and noncash motivators.

Here is a practical project form to use.

HIRING AND TRAINING A PLANNER ASSISTANT

Step or Element	Action Our Company Will Take
Knowledge	
Expectations	
Work with others	
Preparations	
Follow-through	
Planning defined	
Time investment	
Job description	
Specification for planner	
Screening	
Orienting planner	
Orienting executives	
Explanation	
Demonstration	
Practical work	
Coaching	
Independence	
Touch base	
Corrections	
Final action	
Incentives	

Follow this training program, and you will have a good, productive planner, who will help you to enjoy the results of a highly effective program.

Part IV

Checklists, Final Questions, and Selling the Plan

24

Start-up Checklist:
Personal Questions

Words and ideas are the only things that last forever.

— Hazlitt

Ideas are more permanent than people.

— Vanbee

This section is designed for people who are beginning a new enterprise. The goal here is to give you a number of questions to answer, which eventually can help you and your business.

These are the same questions that are asked by leading management consultants charging $2,000 a day. They focus in on areas that are most likely to cause failure or success, depending on how you answer them. You may have already covered many of these issues, but beginning ventures almost never remember to cover all of them. One missed item can cause failure.

These questions are short, brief, condensed and clear, not lengthy or vague. They cover key personal elements that most plans books ignore. Yet your success has a great deal to do with you as a person: your skills, habits, background, and personality. These questions also trigger new questions, thoughts, ideas, and channels of inquiry. This list is by no means the ultimate. No checklist can cover *every* possibility. This one simply covers most of the key points.

Try to answer these as honestly as you can. If you are not sure, ask yourself, "If I asked someone who knows me very well, what answer would they give?" Honest answers can save you a world of hurts. Don't expect to bat one thousand. Nobody's perfect. If you know your weak spots, you can protect yourself more effectively.

START-UP QUESTIONS

Why Do You Want to Begin This Venture?

	YES	NO
1. To escape a treadmill grind?		
2. To control your life?		
3. To prove something to yourself?		
4. To prove something to others?		
5. To live up to people's expectations?		
6. To get rich, quick?		
7. To gain independence from others?		
8. To gain excitement?		
9. Just for the hell of it?		
10. Desparation—no job?		
11. Because it's easier than a job?		
12. On a dare?		
13. On a hunch?		
14. Because it's a family tradition?		

15. To make more money? _____ _____

16. To earn by filling a known need? _____ _____

17. Because you have a habit of initiative? _____ _____

18. Because you respond well to challenges? _____ _____

The first twelve reasons are not very good. The last six reasons may point to success. Owning a small business usually takes *many* more hours per week than a job. Ask anyone who runs one. Yes, you do have more control, but you also have far more responsibilities. With many owners, the business controls them. Proving something is fine, but not by itself. There should be other reasons. And there are far cheaper, quicker, and easier ways to gain excitement. People who have difficulty getting the job they want rarely do well as a business owner, but there are exceptions to this. Above all remember that running a business is very hard work.

DO YOU HAVE THE KAPCA SUCCESS FORMULA?

Specialists in start-ups find that those who succeed usually have five key characteristics or traits:

1. Knowledge through both formal training and on-the-job experience.

2. Attitude or willingness to work hard for long hours for many months and usually some years, living on a low income. Start-ups take years to become profitable; eighty percent never show a profit.

3. Plans are a vital part of success. A business without a plan is a ship without a rudder.

4. Capital (cash or other resources, borrowed or invested). Few businesses can start on $10. Most start-ups need at least $100,000, but not all. Some start with $10,000.

5. The final A is for Action, putting the program into effect: KAPCA, or Knowledge, Attitude, Plan, Capital, Action.

KAPCA Questions

	Yes	No
1. Do you have knowledge by training?	_____	_____
by experience?	_____	_____
2. An attitude for long hours, for years?	_____	_____
3. Plan (SWOT)?	_____	_____
4. Capital such as cash, talent, other resources?	_____	_____
5. Action to put plan into effect?	_____	_____

If you have few or none of these, you are very unlikely to succeed. If you have all (or nearly all) of these, you are much more likely to succeed.

MORE START-UP QUESTIONS

Do you know yourself pretty well?

	Yes	No
1. Do you like to guide and direct?	_____	_____
2. Can you make good choices?	_____	_____
3. Will people follow your directions?	_____	_____
4. Can you compete well?	_____	_____
5. Do you have good self-control?	_____	_____
6. Do people call you determined?	_____	_____
7. Do you schedule and manage time well?	_____	_____
8. Do you arrange action toward goals?	_____	_____
9. Do you enjoy working with others?	_____	_____

10. Do others enjoy working with you? _____ _____

11. Have you worked 60-hour weeks recently? _____ _____

12. Can you handle emotional stress? _____ _____

13. Will your family give full support? _____ _____

14. Can your nerves handle a failed venture? _____ _____

Does your training and background fit?

1. Have you a list of abilities needed? _____ _____

2. Do you have all or most of these? _____ _____

3. Have you been a unit director? _____ _____

4. If so, were you successful? _____ _____

5. Do you have work experience in this field? _____ _____

6. Do you have formal training in this field? _____ _____

7. Will you get trained before you start? _____ _____

Do your prospects want your product or service?

1. Do you know who your prospects are? _____ _____

2. Do you know where and how many? _____ _____

3. Do you know total dollar market spending? _____ _____

4. Have you discussed product idea with prospects? _____ _____

5. Do they say they need it? _____ _____

6. Do they say they want it? _____ _____

7. Did they suggest improvements? _____ _____

8. If so, did you make these? _____ _____

9. Do you have a realistic sales estimates? _____ _____

10. Is this a good time to enter the market? _____ _____

11. Will you compete well on product/price? _____ _____

12. Do you have a marketing plan prepared? _____ _____

13. Is yours better than those of
    alternate products? _____ _____

Have you avoided legal problems?

1. Is your business name safe? Legal? _____ _____

2. Are you a sole proprietorship? _____ _____

3. If so, do you know you personally
   can be sued? _____ _____

4. Are you a partnership? _____ _____

5. Do you know that you both can be
   sued equally? _____ _____

6. Is your business a corporation? _____ _____

7. Do you know a corporation protects
   you personally? _____ _____

8. Do you know the cost of being incorporated? _____ _____

9. Can you afford this? _____ _____

10. Do you need a license to do business? _____ _____

11. Are you aware of key statutes? _____ _____

12. Are there laws about signs? Snow removal? _____ _____

13. Will you be in compliance with laws on:

    Environmental protection? _____ _____

    Taxes (city, state, federal)? _____ _____

Withholding tax requirements? _____ _____

Social Security withholding? _____ _____

Workmen's Compensation? _____ _____

OSHA regulations? _____ _____

14. Do you have contact with a lawyer? _____ _____

15. Has a lawyer reviewed your plans? _____ _____

16. Do you have good insurance for life, health, fire, theft, and liability? _____ _____

Do you have a good location?

1. Do you have easy access for customers? _____ _____

2. Do facilities need remodeling? _____ _____

3. Do you need furniture and fixtures? _____ _____

4. Can you afford remodeling? Fixtures? _____ _____

5. Are you renting, not buying? _____ _____

6. Can rent apply to purchase, if need be? _____ _____

7. Is parking adequate? Clean? Lighted? _____ _____

Do you have good suppliers?

1. Do you have a product line? Services? _____ _____

2. Do you know what inventory you need? _____ _____

3. Do you have suppliers for all you need? _____ _____

4. Did you check their customers' opinions? _____ _____

5. Did you check their competitors? _____ _____

Do you plan for proper documents?

1. Will you account for costs? Sales? _____   _____

2. Bills to pay? Vouchers due to you? _____   _____

3. Profits and losses, by month? _____   _____

4. Pay due employees? Withholding? _____   _____

5. Do you have an accountant? _____   _____

What about your personal income?

1. Do you have cash in the bank? _____   _____

2. Do you have any other income? _____   _____

3. Does spouse have an income? _____   _____

4. Do you know your total living needs? _____   _____

5. Do you have enough income
   to meet these? _____   _____

6. Do you know when business will profit? _____   _____

7. Can you meet personal needs until then? _____   _____

8. Do you have an emergency (money) plan? _____   _____

9. Can you handle failure (financially)? _____   _____

10. Have you ever been bankrupt? _____   _____

11. Have you discussed your venture
    with your banker? _____   _____

If you answer all of these questions in a positive or favorable way, you chances of success are good. But you could still fail, through circumstances beyond your control. Some examples: severe new competition, major cost increases, drops in demand, new adverse laws, union action, health problems, and other difficulties. Those are the risks you take.

If you have answered negatively, unfavorably, or adversely on even a few of the above questions, your danger increases proportionately. Make plans to correct those items or protect yourself from them. At least you are forewarned and so forearmed. You won't be taken by surprise.

25

Start-Up:

Ten Short Forms To Begin Your Business

Don't tell me why we can't do it, tell me how we can.

—R. Craig

Here is a more complete coverage of the checklist material in an earlier chapter; use the lists below to review key points in more detail when you are considering starting an entirely new business.

COVER

Title: _____

Company name:_____ Date: _____

Address: _____

Manager:_____

Basic idea: _____

1. MARKET SITUATION

Is Our Idea Feasible? (Tests)

(__) 1. Affordable? _____ (__) 7. User likes sample?_____

(__) 2. Who buys? _____ (__) 8. Adjust to likes? _____

(__) 3. P & L Forecast? _____ (__) 9. Re-checked? _____

(__) 4. Pays off?_____ (__) l0. Budget made? _____

(__) 5. Customer appeal? _____ (__) 11. Market test?_____

(__) 6. Sample made? _____ (__)12. Expansion? _____

Market Facts

What are we selling? _____

Who's our competitor? _____

Where are our customers?_____

Why will they buy ours? _____

Why are we better? _____

When do they buy? _____

What need do we fill?_____

Remarks:_____

2. WEAPON RESOURCES (COMPANY FACTS)

Key manager: _____ Weaknesses: _____

Key skills: _____ Opportunities: _____

Key experience: _____ Threats: _____

Funds available: _____ Product/service advantages: _____

Strengths: _____

Remarks: _____

3. OBJECTIVES PROFIT/LOSS FORECAST

	Per. 1	Per. 2	Per. 3	Per. 4	Per. 5	Per.6
Sales	____	____	____	____	____	____
Costs	____	____	____	____	____	____
Profit/loss	____	____	____	____	____	____
Cumulative P/L	____	____	____	____	____	____

Remarks: _____

4. MARKET PLAN

Product _____ Promotion _____

Price _____ Person Selling _____

Package _____ Physical Distribution _____

Premium _____ Publicity _____

Advertising _____

Remarks: _____

5. PRODUCTION PLAN

Protect idea: _____

(__)Patent _____ (__)Copyright_____

(__)Trademark _____ (__)Servicemark_____

(Best protection is simple discretion. Don't talk too much. Loose lips sink ships. Show ideas only to a few, quality people.)

(__) Design _____ (__)Product inventory_____

(__) "Shop" suppliers _____ (__)Start date _____

(__) Production costs _____ (__)Volume_____

Remarks: _____

6. FINANCE PLAN (FINDING THE MONEY)

Best: Own cash _____ Borrow on home/insurance _____

Loan: friend/family _____ SBA guaranteed loan_____

Friends buy shares _____ Credit from supplier _____

Loan from bank _____ Venture capital group_____

Remarks: _____

7. PEOPLE PLAN (Stay at a minimum staff at first)

(__)Family help _____ (__)Job qualifications: _____

(__)Clerk (temp) _____ (__)Duties: _____

(__)Partner _____ (__)Training:_____

Remarks: _____

8. OUTSIDER PLAN (Advice Givers)

(__) Banker: _____   (__)Mentor/friend: _____

(__) Lawyer: _____   (__)Supplier: _____

(__) Accountant: _____   (__)SBA free counselors: _____

Remarks: _____

9. SELLING THE PLAN (To Money Sources)

(__)Prepare _____   (__)Give plan summary _____

(__)Explain it _____   (__) Answer questions _____

(__)Show values _____   (__)Stay pleasant _____

(__)Show $ goals _____   (__) Ask for OK_____

Remarks: _____

10. TIME PLAN (Next 3 key steps to take)

	Who	Does what	When
1.	_____	_____	_____
2.	_____	_____	_____
3.	_____	_____	_____

26

Preparation:

Facts, Payout, And Tactics

Luck is what happens when preparation meets opportunity.
— Stephen Leacock

"Just get me the money. I'll do the rest," say some managers. Sometimes they are right. They are so skilled, so seasoned, so well proved that they almost can't miss. This applies to some managers. Others just say it, but can't produce. The challenge facing the investor is to know which is which and who is who. And there are ways of doing this.

The purpose of this section is to review those ways. To help you get ready, so that your efforts pay off and you reach your financial plan goals: You raise the money.

We will see that there are basically three steps you can take to prepare for meeting with the money people:

1. have a good plan backed by thorough preparation,

2. know the right sources, and

3. make a strong written and personal presentation.

This section will warn you of problems and point you toward the best opportunities and methods for securing financial support.

Your situation

Clearly you need capital, either equity or debt (or both).

If you have read this far, and followed most of the preceding material, then you already have many things going for you. For one thing, you know how much money you need, and why. You will also have facts, goals, and tactical plans.

In these next few chapters, we will look at where the money is and how you can get it through good presentations.

Start with a good business plan

A business plan has at least two key purposes. Number one is to manage limited resources so that they maximize your income (or at least minimize your losses). Number two is to obtain capital financing by convincing people to loan you money as debt capital or to buy your stock, providing you with equity capital. Some plans books emphasize this financing function, perhaps because that can be the major challenge for managers. But in making this financing emphasis, the implication is that getting the money is the first step. This is usually not true.

Managers who *first* generate an excellent plan for use as a management tool have a far easier time getting financed than managers with a poor plan. Good plans lead to good financing; going after financing without a comprehensive plan can lead to disaster. To dramatize this point, just change places with the financier for a moment. If two managers came to you seeking capital, one with an excellent plan and one with little or nothing, which would you favor?

Remember, money people don't judge you on your baby blue eyes or your enthusiasm; they want to know about the safety of their investment, how much money they can make and what the chances of success are. They play the odds and favor those with a good plan.

Is a plan designed to manage resources or get financing? It is to do both. But management comes first. The earlier sections in this document were designed to help you manage toward a profit. But here we now will look at using that management tool as a financial generator.

What are your weapons?

Your SWOT formula. Your situation chart (where you analyzed your market). Your weapons resource chart (where you reviewed your company). Your objectives chart (where you set out your goals for sales and profits and image, long-and short-term). Then your Mark-Prod-Fin-POST strategy formula (plans for marketing, production, finance, people, outsiders, selling the plan, and time planning). (The selling plan is introduced later.)

Your objectives should be very clear

Know just what you want and what you will request. Are you looking for a loan or are you selling stock? And how many dollars are you requesting? Be clear about this. Don't pussyfoot around. (Entrepreneurs have come to me, a modest financier, looking for capital, and yet have never told me whether they wanted to sell stock or get a loan, or how many dollars or how soon or for what. They probably knew, but simply didn't make this clear!)

This section on preparation need not be very long, because we have already covered nearly all of the key elements in a good plan. You now have most or nearly all the weapons prepared.

Your best tactics from here, in using your management plan to approach financiers effectively, is largely one of fine tuning your preparation.

This means you should expand the financial elements in three ways: a spending schedule, a prominent payout plan, and specific tailoring. As a fourth item, you should minimize length. Let's look at each of those four steps.

First Include a list of expected spending or investment by item, showing dollar amounts, suppliers, dates, and purpose. Investors want to know exactly how the money will be used and why. They especially want to know that you know, that you have a plan even if they don't understand the technology on some of the items to be purchased. Without such a list, investors get the uncomfortable feeling that they may be providing too much or too little and all without any control.

Second Be sure the profit and loss cash flow projection is in fairly good detail, as accurate and realistic as possible and included in the front of the plan (probably in the executive summary).

Third Tailor your presentation (written and oral) to fit your audience. Suggestions: Equity capital people (stock buyers) are especially interested in good, sound feasibility studies. Summarize any such opinion surveys, user studies, or market tests.

Equity investors, especially the early or start-up ones, want to believe that the enterprise will not only survive and prosper, but that they can sell out and make about a 50 percent return per year on their investment.

Debt capital people (lenders) are interested in conserving and protecting capital and making repayments. Include a repayment schedule.

Both want to know that the company is well managed, knows the market, has specific strengths, specific objectives (SWOT) and has a set of tactical plans (Mark-Prod-Fin-Post). Both debt and equity investors tend to be optimists, but cautious optimists, since they've usually been burned a few times by being unrealistic.

Fourth Managers and financiers want and need plans, but they don't want a Dickens novel or telephone book. Some planners think bulk stands for merit. This may be true for their own personal use, but is *not* the case when selling to financiers. Most of them see hundreds of proposals. They rarely give a plan more than a five-minute scan, and then they make their judgment (sometimes to invest, more often to get more information). Be sure to have a good executive summary that can be read in a few minutes. Three to six pages is about right. It should be condensed, factual, touching all key points. The remaining plan can be thirty to fifty pages or even more, giving information that backs up and expands on the summary.

If you have covered these items in your written or oral presentation, you will be in an excellent position to take the next key steps: locating your money sources and then presenting, selling, and obtaining your financing.

27

Money Sources

Patience is a necessary ingredient to genius.

— B. Disraeli

There are lots of money sources. Many either charge high interest rates or want a part of the business, or both. Often they are hard to find, take a long time deciding, are very selective, or can help only a few firms. Only you can decide when the price is worth the service. But in any case, don't be hesitant to inquire. If you are well prepared you have no need to be timid, reluctant, or shy.

This section will summarize the various dollar sources. You can then match up your wants and needs with the various suppliers (almost like a catalog money store). You pick what you like best and what fits your corporate body.

There are at least sixteen common sources of money. These include your own savings, family, friends, the bank, venture capital groups, going public, SBIC's, Farmers Home Administration, the

SBA, nonbank lenders, the SBIR, an angel, hidden sources, BDCs, state help, and the EDA.

Two kinds of capital exist: debt and equity. You should be aware that these two kinds of capital mean two kinds of obligations and benefits.

Debt means borrowed money. The advantage is that you have rapidly available funds. The disadvantage is that the capital not only must be repaid but, in addition, you must also pay interest. (Some people borrow $100,000 and then splurge because they think they are wealthy! Actually they have never been poorer. They not only must repay the $100,000 (perhaps at $10,000 a year), but must also pay the interest (maybe another $10,000 a year). They now owe $20,000 a year that they did not owe before they borrowed. That also means that their business must generate a lot more than this each year just to pay the debt.

Equity means owning a part of the business. The main advantage is that you don't need to repay anything. You and the stockholders share in the fortune or failure of the firm. Usually, you are much better off to put up the money yourself, if you can. The disadvantage is simply that you may not have enough personal assets to provide the needed equity financing.

If your son starts a lemonade stand and needs $100, he may borrow $40 from Mom. This is debt. If he and Dad each put in $30 as shareholders, that's equity. In total, that generates the $100 needed. If the operation prospers, the $40 loan is paid off and the two owners split the profits. If the operation bombs, and is liquidated at a total of, let's say, $60, then $40 goes to Mom, to pay off the debt. That leaves only $20. This is split between the two owners. Since they each put up $30, they each see a loss of $20. Note that *the debt is paid first*. What remains, goes to the owners. This is oversimplified, but the points are valid.

Following are the main sources of money for your business.

1. *Your personal savings.* This money usually becomes equity or ownership. In the example above, you might put in the entire $100. No debt is involved. This is usually pretty clear, clean, and simple. Unfortunately, it is usually not enough to launch the enterprise. Most new enterprises need $100,000 to $200,000; few people have that much cash available. However, most new ventures that branch off

from established firms are financed in a way similar to this, from currently available assets.

2. *Your family.* One member of your family might loan money (like Mom above). But others, like Dad, may prefer to take an equity (or ownership) position. But even then, in the real world, this may be far too little to provide the $100,000 or $200,000 needed.

3. *Friends* might also provide debt and equity capital, but again, $200,000 is difficult to accumulate from such sources.

4. *Your bank* is often your best bet for the rest of the package. Most banks are very happy to make you a loan, if it is small, short-term, backed with lots of collateral, and is for a successful, on-going business. Then the bank is safe. You are fairly likely to repay in the short term, say, sixty days, and if you don't they can take your collateral. Cruel? Not really. After all, they are lending out their depositors' funds and must guard these very, very carefully. Start-ups are especially dangerous, since some 80 percent fail in five years. Yet, generally, banks can only stand a 1 percent to 2 percent loss on bad loans. Most banks, like the other sources listed here, have been burned with loans that were never repaid. Loan officers, who tend to have families to support like the rest of us, are fired. This is not much fun. They learn bitter lessons. Unfortunately, if you need to borrow $100,000 or $200,000 to start a small business, you probably cannot repay it within sixty days. You need a much longer term loan, more like six years. Further, you may not have a nice house, yacht, or family farm that will serve as collateral for a loan of that size. In short, the bank may not be much help for a large, long-term, unsecured, start-up loan.

5. *A venture capital group.* These are people who may have a few hundred thousand dollars available, money they would like to invest in a small business. They may be looking for a company like yours. They might be glad to put up $100,000 or $200,000 or much more.

   Of course, they have a price. First, they usually want equity (not lender) status. They want ownership. Second, they usually want controlling ownership (51 percent or more). And they want to see an annual return of 40 percent to 50 percent on their money. That's about like paying 45 percent interest. These investors want to know: How much can I make? lose? Can I get out of the deal? And who says the product and people are any good? They are tough cookies. They will ask, "Who do you know, who are your people, who do you work for, and what is your package?" They are especially interested in the cash flow and break-even point. They often look at 50 to 200 proposals before picking one. If you have a very high profit opportunity, they might be your best source. If not, they may be a hard sell.

6 *Going public.* Here you offer for sale shares of stock in the company for purchase by the public. You are raising equity money, of course, not debt, and you are giving up some ownership. Most firms try to do this by selling less than 50 percent of the firm, thus retaining control themselves.

Often, however, this does not generate enough capital. Often, firms must sell more than half, and apparently lose control to stockholders. This may not be as bad as it sounds, since few of the other (public) shareholders may own more than 10% and the original owners may hold 40%, remaining the largest minority stockholders. Many firms are controlled with a much smaller portion than this. The public offering procedure can be fairly complex. Your best bet is to contact your lawyer and banker. Various booklets are available free or at low cost.

7. *The SBIC* (or Small Business Investment Corporation). They are government-backed, flexible financing devices designed to provide both equity and long-term funds to both urban and rural small firms. They are licensed by the SBA, and are privately owned and operated. They get their capital from private investors and the government. They make loans or buy stock; loans may be unsecured or not fully collateralized. The SBIC may be a subsidiary of a private, separate, profit-making firm.

These institutions were organized to provide financing to small firms having difficulty obtaining capital. They also provide management counsel and have some good tax advantages.

234 • Strategic Planning for the Small Business

The disadvantages are that the SBIC is very selective in making an investment, and there is an average of less than $2 million available per state. That's enough to finance about 20 small ventures at $100,000 each. Yet there are an average of 12,000 new starts per state and 280,000 existing small business per state. These institutions, in fact, can finance only about 1 business in every 14,000.

8. *The Small Business Administration* is an agency of the Federal government. It has two major services: finance and management counseling. It was designed to help small firms obtain long-term bank loans by guaranteeing the loan to the bank, thus protecting the bank and making them more willing to provide the debt funds. (More details on this are provided in the next chapter.)

9. *The Farmer's Home Administration* (FmHa) provides services similar to those of the SBA, but can guarantee much larger loans, up to $33 million, averaging $900,000. FmHa has a minimum equity requirement of only 10 percent. They have 1,800 county offices, and so are highly accessible.

10. *Other nonbank lenders* include Money Store Investment Corporation, Springfield, NJ (201) 467-9000. They offer guaranteed loans in twelve different states. Merrril Lynch Small Business Lending Company serves all states with offices in most major cities. (Check your local directory for the number.) ITT Small Business Finance Corporation, Minneapolis, MN (612) 540-8509, provides loans nationally.

11. *Small Business Innovation Research* (SBIR) is a federal program. It requires federal agencies with large research and development budgets to devote about 1 percent of this to help with small business research. Generally, the large agency has a list of products they need. They make this list available on request. If a small firm (normally very high-tech), feels they can provide one of these products, they make a comprehensive scientific proposal. The advantage is that if approved, the proposer can win a grant of $30,000 to $50,000 for further research. This is not a loan or stock purchase, but a conditional gift. If that research proves satisfactory, the company might get a second grant ten times the initial amount. As a third benefit, the company

may end up with a final product that not only is purchased in large quantities by the large government agency, but is also marketable to the private sector.

The disadvantages are that the funds are purely for research, not for company management purposes. This is not a program to help small retailers, manufacturers, or services start up standard or routine business operations. Second, it is normally for very high-tech operations only. Third, the proposal usually must be comprehensive, technical, detailed, advanced, and quite sophisticated. Fourth, even then, only a very small percent of the proposals are accepted. Fifth, what is at issue is usually a proposal for solving a very specific, designated technical government need. This is not funding for a new idea that the company created and thinks the government just might want. Finally, most initial grants go no further and do not win the larger funds.

One author used TV to advertise his book indicating that the government has huge grants for anyone who wants them; readers were instructed not to take no for an answer. You can see that he is perhaps technically part right, but making a major exaggeration, to put it mildly. The Federal Trade Commission has filed a complaint.

12. *An angel or financial backer* is usually a person who has access to substantial funds. He or she may have a desire to help small business start-ups or expansion with substantial debt or equity capital, or both. The backer may sit on the board of directors and play an active role in management of the firm. Often the backer is doing the same thing with numerous companies, and so brings a wealth of skills, knowledge, and experience.

There are some disadvantages here. First, such people are usually hard to find. Second, they often have far more financial requests than you can reasonably accommodate. Third, they may not have *enough* funds to do the job or, fourth, want to take over too large a share of the company, leaving the original founders with almost no ownership or control. In effect, the former owners become employees and extreme minority shareholders. Fifth, even as a large minority shareholder, the backer may hold a large enough portion of the stock to control the company or to insist upon dominating company operations.

13. *Hidden sources.* Sometimes a part of the company's assets, rights, inventories, or prepayments can be converted to capital. For example, you may be able to raise cash by selling off unneeded land or buildings, or selling these even if they are needed, and then leasing them back, thus freeing up cash. Many companies tie up far too much capital in big truck fleets, machines, land, bricks, and mortar, so that the firm has no funds available for tools, inventory, salaries, marketing, or other such items. They should decide whether they really want to be in the trucking/real estate business. Sometimes the company owns some patents, foreign rights, franchises, or licensing arrangements that they no longer want or need and can sell to another firm. Some firms, too, have paid high taxes on large profits in preceding years, but show a sharp loss in the current year. In that case they might be able to average out their profits and obtain a tax refund. Net result: more capital.

14. *Business Development Corporations* (BDCs). These groups are exempt from some parts of the 1940 Investment Company Act, and so have added freedom to invest. On the other hand they must keep a large portion of their portfolio in securities that cannot be purchased on margin, they must give proven management counsel to their portfolio companies, and most of their board must be outsiders, holding only a small percentage of the BDC stock. Other than that, they act largely the same as a venture capital group.

15. *State departments of economic development.* Nearly every state has programs to assist business start-ups, expansion, or firms that want to move into the state and need capital for operating, equipment, or fixed assets. These funds are either loaned directly to the company or represent back-up funds to support guaranteed bank loans. For example, the bank makes a loan to the company, but it is guaranteed by the state. If the company defaults, the state covers any loss. Sometimes the state even gives the capital to the company

as a grant to encourage the firm to move into the state. (Some firms move several times, just to get these grants. Perhaps this is not all bad, but it is not very ethical, either.)

16. *The Economic Development Administration* (EDA) is a federal government program to help economically depressed areas. The government has designated many counties in the country as depressed. Companies in those counties may be eligible for a federal loan. Most of these loans are under one million dollars. Generally, the EDA requires the business to provide a portion of the financing as equity funding before a loan will be made.

Where to find these people. Your best bet is to check with one or more of these six sources: your local banker, lawyer, SBA, the local chamber of commerce, the yellow pages, or your CPA. If these sources don't know the exact name, address, or phone number, they can usually refer you to someone who does know.

28

The Small Business Administration

Recognition gravitates to those who can—and it flows away from those who can't.

— Appley

This chapter is devoted entirely to the SBA because this agency, one of the smallest branches of the federal government, is vitally important in financing small businesses. There are about 14 million small businesses in the U.S. eligible for SBA services. True, most small firms start with total capital of less than $50,000 and get the entire amount from personal savings, friends, family or as new ventures branching off from existing businesses. Only a small percentage of start-ups get SBA loans. Most SBA loans are for on-going expansion, not start-ups.

But, of the small businesses that have no other recourse except long-term bank loans, the SBA helps about 35 percent. The remainder is serviced by many other groups. In other words, the SBA is far and away the largest single source of long-term business loans.

This chapter will give you an overview of the help you can ask for and get from the SBA, often free of charge.

Small business makes up over half of our economy, and many more such firms start up every year. The SBA is the country's largest provider of long-term business loans, usually arranging around $100,000 for seven to ten years. Most of these loans are actually made by the bank, at normal interest rates, but with up to 90 percent of the loan guaranteed by the SBA. To be eligible, you must be of good character, a small business, operate for profit, and show good repayment ability. Banks usually ask you to provide about 25 percent to 50 percent of the total funds needed, with the bank lending you the rest. There are many common misconceptions about the SBA: that it is mostly for minorities, that it provides very low interest, direct loans, that it serves only a percent or two of businesses (mostly bankruptcies) and that it offers few other services besides lending. All of these are untrue.

The SBA likes to explain to small firms how they fit into our economy. About 93 percent of all firms are small businesses. Small businesses employ more than half of the U.S. labor force and provides about 70 percent of all new innovations and new jobs. Over half a million new companies start each year. A survey in *USA Today* indicated that about 40 percent of the adult U.S. population has a private dream of starting their own businesses.

In the last few years, more women than men opened businesses. These were mostly in the service industry. Since the SBA started in 1953, it has guaranteed loans to about 1.5 million companies. This represents over 10 percent of the total companies now in business and over $40 billion in guaranteed loans. In some towns, every small businesses on Main Street or in the shopping mall has received some kind of SBA help.

Each year, the SBA guarantees loans worth about $4 billion, representing about 50,000 separate loans. And each year, the SBA trains or counsels, on a person-to-person basis, about 500,000 people. For each loan made, about ten people are counseled.

In some states, 30 percent of the businesses get SBA help every month. Much of this help is provided by SBA management information. About 90 percent of the people serving the SBA are volunteers who work without pay. (Fifteen thousand retired executives and 15,000 senior business college students.) Few government agencies can say this.

In thousands of cases, major U.S. businesses never would have existed at all without the SBA. Many of these firms went on to become giants. (Examples: Winnebago, Apple Computer, Nike shoes, Federal Express, Godfather Pizza, and many others.) Remember, with or without an SBA loan, nearly every giant business in the world started out as a small business.

From the SBA you might get a long-term loan, when there may be no other source. A second key benefit is the wealth of management counsel available to you, with or without a loan. There is little or no charge either for the financing help or management help. Some of this assistance is worth many thousands of dollars. SBA also provides help getting Federal government contracts and surety bonds. They assist with special groups such as veterans, women, exporters, minorities, and the handicapped, and they provide over one hundred low-cost booklets and films. However, most people getting SBA services are fairly average citizens, not members of these special groups.

The following questions are the ones most commonly asked by the thousands of SBA applicants each year.

Where do I get the money?
Many people have been led to believe that the money comes from the SBA. Actually, it is a bank that makes the loan and provides the funds. The SBA guarantees appropriate loans.

What are my chances of getting a loan?
That depends on your qualifications and quality of your application. During some months, many SBA offices approve much more than half of the applications sent by the bank.

What are the types of SBA loans?
The agency has about one hundred offices across the country and is probably best known for direct loans to small firms at low interest. This was a major program at one time, but no longer. Today, nearly

all SBA loans are guaranteed bank loans. For example, if your business needs to get a long-term loan of $100,000, you might go to your local bank. If they will make the loan, you don't need the SBA. But suppose they say, "We'd like someone to guarantee your loan, to pay it off, in case you can't. Do you have an Aunt Suzy or an Uncle Sam who might cosign for you?" The SBA might become the Uncle Sam, and is mainly a guarantor to help you get the loan.

What are the loan making mechanics?

The bank has SBA applications or can get them quickly. You are supposed to fill it out, although most bankers will help (or you can use your accountant). Or, for a fee, there are services that will do this for you. When your application is completed, the bank sends it to the SBA.

What should be included in the application?

There are blank forms for you to provide:

projected earnings (pay-out plan),

a list of collateral,

your (brief) personal history,

how the loan will be used,

how the loan will be repaid,

the company balance sheet and profit and loss sheet,

your personal financial statement,

your training and experience, and

other related items, like a buy-out agreement, and a business plan.

How soon will I have a decision?

On a properly completed loan application, a decision is usually made and the bank informed within ten days. Most long delays are caused by incomplete or error-filled applications.

Who is eligible?

Generally any for-profit U.S. company that is classified as a small business. The agency almost never makes bail-out loans for a bankrupt business. You need not be turned down by a bank to become eligible, although you may be wise to check several banks to find the best arrangement.

How is "small business" defined?

There are hundreds of size standards, but as a rule of thumb, companies with under 500 employees and under $2 million in annual sales are considered small. If you are well under these, you probably are eligible. There are many exceptions above these limits. If you are near or over these, a phone call to the SBA will clarify the matter.

How does the SBA decide? With what credit criteria?

Generally the applicant must be: for-profit, small, of good character, not bankrupt, able to manage the business, able to repay the loan, and able to put some other funds into the business. The SBA will rarely provide 100 percent of the financing, except in cases where the applicant already has made a substantial investment, such as a new dental school graduate.

Ability to repay is probably the key factor in most SBA decisions. Here is where they may look for your Knowledge, Attitude, Plans, Capital, and Action program. They seek formal and on-the-job training as an ideal combination of knowledge. They look for people who show a willingness to work fifty or sixty hours a week for some years, at low income, since that is usually what it takes. They seek a good business plan, with special emphasis on a realistic cash flow forecast and good market feasibility (as demonstrated in this book), and just as almost any other capital supplier wants.

How much can you borrow? How much will you be asked to put down?

The SBA can guarantee up to 90 percent of a loan up to $750,000. Most loans are for about $100,000.There is no fixed percent of the total package that the SBA will supply or expect you to supply. But as a general rule, the SBA likes to see you put up one-fourth to one-half. For example, if the total package or program needs $200,000 in capital, the SBA would like to see you put up $100,000 as equity capital, and they will put up (guarantee) $100,000 in debt capital.

If that is not possible, but you can put up $50,000, they might put up the remaining $150,000. On special occasions, such as the case of the dentist, they might be happy if you put in only $10,000 or even $1,000. But this is very rare.

The SBA sometimes walks a fine line. They are using public funds to guarantee a loan, and so are very anxious to be sure that the public money is protected. On the other hand, they are guaranteeing a loan to the public and want to be sure that everyone who qualifies is well served. They are sometimes in a no win situation, where neither public is pleased. But generally, both are well satisfied.

Are SBA loans low interest?
Yes, a few are. But most are not. Remember, it is the bank that makes the loan. The SBA only guarantees it. The bank sets the interest rate. The SBA can guarantee a loan if it is 2 ¾% over prime or less. Any loans with interest above that are not eligible for SBA help. The few direct, low-interest SBA loans are for special situations, such as disaster damage.

How soon must I pay off the loan?
The terms usually run from seven to twenty years.

What about collateral?
Banks are generally most interested in collateral, as a quick dollar source in case of trouble. The SBA is mainly interested in repayment ability.

How does the SBA protect the bank?
The agency guarantees up to 90 percent of the loan. For example, if the bank makes an SBA guaranteed loan of $100,000, and the next month the borrower goes totally broke, the SBA buys back the loan from the bank for $90,000. In this case, the most the bank can lose is $10,000. If, however, the loan is mostly paid off, or the company has a high liquidation value, perhaps through expensive inventory (such as diamonds), the company might be sold and the bank would lose far less than $10,000. (In fact, the sale might even cover the total loan.)

Why does helping the bank serve you, the borrower?
Because offering such protection to the bank means that they are more willing to make the loan. Without such guarantees, many or most long-term, small business loans would not be made.

Do I really need to repay an SBA loan?
You are definitely expected to repay the loan to the bank. If you do not, extensive management counsel is sometimes offered, and repayment extensions or new arrangements are made. If the loan is

still not paid off in any way, the bank can ask the SBA to make good on the guarantee and cover the amount due. Some assets or collateral may be sold to help cover the loan. Bankruptcy and even litigation may be necessary.

An SBA guaranteed loan is not a grant or a gift. SBA funds to pay the bank on a defaulted loan are funds provided by the taxpayer and, by law, the SBA must protect these taxpayers as much as practical.

Here are some common misconceptions about the SBA that have caused a lot of false starts, conflicts and heartache.

The SBA

1. is mainly to bail-out bankrupt firms,

2. is mainly for minorities,

3. mainly makes low-interest, direct loans to anyone who wants them and even makes grants if you insist,

4. requires a ton of paperwork beyond normal loans, take months to process, always want over 50 percent down,

5. insists that you must be turned down by three banks, and are usually out of money or lending authority,

6. wants to run your business after making the loan,

7. serves only about 1 percent of businesses, since it just makes loans and provide no other help, has few volunteers, and doesn't care about helping veterans, handicapped people, exporters, rural or young people, and

8. deals only with high-risk firms and will cancel the guarantee at the slightest excuse.

Remember these ideas are mostly or entirely incorrect. They are largely founded on a few exceptions that became newsworthy only because they were unusual things.

For more information, contact your local SBA office or phone the (free) answer desk at 1-800-368-5855.

29

Selling Your Plan

Earnestness is the salt of eloquence.
— Victor Hugo

Our purpose here is to outline practical steps you can use to successfully sell plans to investors. This will entail making an effective presentation.

We will discuss ways to design a strong, high-impact proposal by covering our situation, weapons, objectives, and tactics. Those tactics include preparing facts, planning the logistics or mechanics of a presentation, handouts, tone of voice, financial emphasis, results, visuals, practice, handling challenging questions, responding with the best answers, negotiating to *yes*, outlining the next steps, and making an enthusiastic close that seals the deal.

YOUR PRESENTATION

Now it is time to use your well-designed plan to present, impress and convince your sources to invest capital. We will look at a fairly formal presentation, one that might take fifteen minutes or so, as do most such proposals. If you wish to streamline this to just five minutes, you can simply shorten each item. But avoid totally dropping any point, since each one is there for an important reason.

In this section, we will use the SWOT formula to build our presentation, designed largely but not exclusively for potential financiers. (Of course, the same general approach is easily adapted to lenders.) The SWOT formula will influence our preparation steps. We'll want to recap our situation, weapon resources, objective, and tactics.

Our SWOT formula starts with the situation (problems and opportunities). Our problem is that financial people are skeptical. They have good reasons: most proposals fail. Our challenge is to resolve, eliminate and overcome those doubts.

But we also have opportunities. The finance people have access to major funds, to capital that can make all the difference between our success and failure. In addition, many presenters forget that, secretly, deep down under the financier's tough shell of doubt, burns a bright flame of hope . . . a hope for big dollar returns. Quietly feed that flame. They know that somewhere in that stack of proposals there is a winner. Our job is to use every minute and every word to convince them that you are that winner.

Our weapon resource is a good plan. Correction—not just a good plan, but an outstanding one. Offer a thorough program with lots of evidence pointing to success (such as a well conceived financial plan and solid feasibility tests). A plan that has answers to challenging questions, usually one that is done not by one person but by a team, is a strong weapon resources.

Our objective is to gain acceptance for the proposal. We want to win their attention, interest, desire and action/support—the old AIDA formula.

Our tactics or strategy are covered below. After explaining these points, we will demonstrate them and then provide you with a practical project form.

In general, your most important strategy steps are first, to try to talk to the right people (otherwise it may be all for nothing). Unfortunately, sometimes you have to present your case to some lower-level people and win their support before you can get to the real decision maker.

In addition, be sure you have a well-planned presentation. And finally, be sure you have practiced it several times, so that you appear smooth, confident, polished, and professional. A presenter with a great plan, but who stumbles, fumbles, and falls, will not win much support. Such a presentation reflects badly on management ability.

Seek the Wow! reaction, as in "Wow, that is a terrific plan!" Remember, you are competing. The last few presenters may have done pretty well, but only one of you is going to be selected. You want to do better than just pretty good. You want to be clearly the best.

Practice your presentation several times, until you are almost tired of it. At that point you've probably got it down pat. Now, comments and interruptions won't bother you very much. Also remember that whatever you give to your listeners may be is used by them to make a later presentation. You gain a lot, and arm your representative well, if you design your material so it is easy to explain. Your problem may not be to sell your immediate audience, but for them to sell others.

Tactical Steps to an Effective, Powerful, and Convincing Plans Presentation

1. *Preparation.* Be sure your plan is thorough and complete with each part done well. Any item may be challenged. Have good answers ready. Practice these with a friendly opponent who asks tough questions about each point.

2. *Line up your prospects* from the money sources listed earlier. To whom do you present? To anyone who might have the funds you need, or who might know such people. When in doubt, present anyway. You never know where it might lead you. Resources develop in unexpected places. If nothing else, you gain practice, and perhaps a supporter and friend.

3. *Plan a quality presentation.* Try to arrange for good, around-the-room introductions, if practical. Begin by passing out a

clear and complete half-page agenda. Investors don't like surprises and usually are pleased to know that you really do, in fact, have a short, well-thought-out program for them. They are less likely to feel that they are wasting their time. Also, they are more likely to let you present the whole program, and this will increase your stature and impact.

4. *The agenda* should show the plan title, people involved, phone numbers, perhaps ten subjects, and the time each person will need to speak. Keep it well paced: not too fast, not too long. Five to fifteen minutes, total, is the best length. Design the program for two or three presenters, but be flexible enough for just one. Divide the time between speakers, if practical; use people who articulate clearly and in a friendly manner. Have a leader who opens and closes. The "supporting players" provide important strength. Investors like to know the concern is not a one-man band, but they do want to deal with the leader. Arrange good mechanics: equipment, flipcharts, handouts, documents, and closing.

5. *Stay simple.* Know your audience interests. Speak loudly enough. Stay flexible, change your pace occasionally, and use short words and personalized phrasing. Let them know they are welcome to ask questions at any point, and that you will have time for these at the end. Listeners like to hear that. Use short stories and examples to make your points; they like that, too.

6. *Use your tone of voice effectively.* Show respect and sincerity, regardless of the audience level or authority. During the presentation, address key people by their names, if you know them. Try to make every word say, "Here is a capable, open, straight-shooting manager I can trust." Never appear devious, cute, uncertain, or unprofessional.

7. *Start friendly, stay friendly.* Talk in terms of others' problems, their goals, procedures, and interests. They don't really care much about yours. This builds attention, interest, desire, and action.

8. *Emphasize financial factors.* These include sales, profits, loan-repayment plans. Show how much is needed in loans

or stock sales. Show why people will buy your product or service. Give as much evidence as possible (feasibility studies, market opinion, use, and sales tests). Dedicate every word and statement to the idea that the plan is solid, sound, and will happen. Relieve fears and doubts.

9. *Emphasize results, not methods.* Finance people are not very interested in the systems to be used in marketing, production, technology, or personnel. A brief statement on each of these is usually enough. Expand on key points if questions are asked, of course.

10. *Use AIDA and SWOT to sell.* Use every reasonable step and fact to get their attention, interest, desire, action. Cover your situation, weapon resources, objectives, tactics/strategy.

11. *Use color slides or a simple flip chart to cover these points.* If you are visiting with a group of five to fifty people, such as a venture group, then good-quality color slides or overheads can be very effective. Or you can use a neat, colorful flip chart of about 18" x 24". Hit the ten highlights of the plan. For a presentation to just one person or a small group, have a flip chart of about half that size, perhaps in a small, stand-up, three-ring binder with 8 ½" x 11" pages in plastic envelopes.

12. *Remember that a smaller chart gives you over a dozen advantages.* It is easy to carry, can be presented almost anywhere (on a plane, at lunch, a car, at a desk), and can be used many times without looking shabby. You may have to go through it five or ten times or more. A flip chart gives you an easy script or track to run on. It also helps you control the presentation and dramatize the plan. It gives your audience something to look at (visuals have more impact than sound), and helps you avoid missing a subject, even if you just brush over it. Flips give you all kinds of flexibility. Interruptions are no problem. You can easily stop, start, skip forward, go back, or repeat.

A flip chart also gives you a tool that any one of your group can use; it even provides your audience something they can take as a selling tool to convince others. A well-employed flip chart usually pleases an audience and can actually stimulate some of them to want to present to others. Now you have a no-cost salesperson, an endorser. Visuals won't substitute for a poor plan, but if they are nicely done, you look professional and you promptly jump ahead of your competition.

13. *Flip chart contents should mention SWOT.* Investors like that sort of strategic thinking. Then highlight the plan. If you have ten key elements or tactical steps, have ten short charts, one on each. Put about five to twenty words on each page, no more. Minimize words. Use bulleted lists of short items. Stay very factual. Anticipate and eliminate problems or questions. Be able to cover each page in under thirty seconds. (Or five seconds, if necessary!)

14. *Have resumes of your key people.* Each should include a good picture and emphasize specific training and successful experience in this field or related ones. One page, one hundred to two hundred words, in large type is ideal. Each one should almost shout competence. Investors like to know the company has willing and able, quality people. Put the resumes in the back of the flip chart.

15. *Have product samples or pictures.* Include sketches or pictures of the building, production line, staff, equipment, package, signs, dealer fact sheets, and in-store displays (or whatever will help you generate confidence). Remember, you may know your product or service like the back of your hand, but your prospective investor may never have heard of it until this minute.

16. *Have summaries of research, feasibility studies, or tests.* Include success stories or testimonial letters from satisfied customers. One short page each. Make no ridiculous claims. Again, build confidence in your competence.

17. *Hand out a copy of the plan.* You might go through it page by page when you have a small group. With a large group, avoid giving it out initially since they will start riffling through it and won't be following your flip-chart presentation. You will have lost them.

18. *Allow ample time for questions, discussion, and answers.* That means if you have fifteen minutes, finish in ten. Then stay as long as you are getting questions.

19. *Answer pleasantly.* Give a short, reasonable answer. If more information is wanted, be ready. But always keep a good, positive tone of voice. "It ain't what you do, it's the way you do it." Use humor or light comments, occasionally.

20. *Stay professional.* Be calm, relaxed with good, quiet self-control. Don't get too casual, jocular, or humorous. It detracts from your plan. People seldom invest in something that others are laughing about.

21. *Get to yes!* Watch listener reactions. If they frown, try to clarify and reinforce the point you are making. If they yawn or look at their watch, speed up. If they want more information or doubt a point, slow down and provide evidence to support it. Sometimes they just want to be sure that you know what you're talking about. Be pleasant and constructive. If that doesn't totally satisfy, offer to come back later with more information.

    Stay cool. Don't argue. Sometimes the question opens an opportunity for you to add another point or two of interest to your listeners. Be ready for that. Emphasize advantages to them; seek acceptance. Try to get them nodding and smiling. And never forget to ask for the order. They expect that. Also, if you can't sign them up, at the very least part with mutual respect and friendship. They may have second thoughts, and there well may be a next time.

22. *Provide a one-page summary of the plan.* Most people won't read the entire business plan, especially if it's more than a few pages.

23. *Make sure handouts include the agenda, plan, a summary, resumes, research summaries, and product samples or service pictures.* Ending without any handouts is a mistake, but giving too many is also not wise. A thirty-page plan and five or six handouts is about right. Offer to send these to anyone they suggest.

24. *Outline the next three priority steps for each part of the business.* For example, Marketing—finalize their plan details, test, and expand. Production—design, test, and deliver. Finance—finish budget details, control costs, and help departments. Manager—prepare, execute, adjust. Work these out by date, activity, and expected results for each department. Show the information on one chart. Investors like to know what will happen next, and that you have planned for this.

25. *Close enthusiastically with a confident, optimistic, determined, sensible, well-planned summary.* Repeat any brief points that your listeners seemed to like. Mention SWOT. Emphasize that the program is well planned, organized, controlled, and proven. Few others can say that. Recap profit projections and the loan repayment schedule or stock value growth possibilities. Mention that market conditions are favorable, goals are realistic, and that solid plans have been made for marketing, production, people, and outside help. Recap the funding needs and time schedule.

    Give your last words with a slight note of urgency and a definite tone of upbeat conviction. Then you might reach over and, with a medium felt pen, sign the flip chart or plan document, as a symbol of your confidence. A summary of about one minute or less is ideal. Choose your words carefully. It may be your last shot.

DEMONSTRATION OF A PLAN FOR
FINANCIAL PRESENTATION

Step Planned	How We Plan to Do Each Step
Prepare strategy plan	SWOT, Mark-Prod-Fin POST elements. Check.
Money sources	Check sources listed and other's advice.
Presentation goals	Approval for $. AIDA. "Wow! Outstanding!"
Presentation date	Two weeks from today, 10 a.m.
Presentation place	Conference room, First National Bank.
Presentation audience	Bank loan officer and stock prospects.
Audience key wants	Safety, assurance of success, profits.
Quality presentation	Well designed. Plan. Handouts. Practiced.
Presentation agenda	People, subjects, timed, question time.
Presenters	Articulate, friendly, skilled, polished.
Finances	Charts on sales, costs, profits, ROI.
Results	Mechanics only briefly to build belief.
Plan summary	Four-page summary as handout with full plan.
Flip chart	Short page on each of ten plan parts.
Samples/or pictures	Samples of product and pictures of use.
Resumes	Picture, training, skills in this field.
Research recap	One-page summary; opinion, use, market tests.
Tone of voice	Pleasant, calm, relaxed, professional.
Humor/serious	A touch of humor, but mostly serious.
Next three steps	Finance, marketing, and production steps.

Getting to yes!	<u>Emphasize audience benefits of each step.</u>
Convincing closing	<u>Confident, plan, control, proven, profits.</u>
Tough questions	<u>Expect challenge on any point. Be ready.</u>
Answers	<u>Short, constructive, pleasant, add points.</u>

FINANCIAL PRESENTATION FORM

Step Planned	How We Plan to Do Each Step
Prepare strategy plan	_____
Money sources	_____
Presentation goals	_____
Presentation date	_____
Presentation place	_____
Presentation Audience	_____
Audience Key Wants	_____
Quality presentation	_____
Presentation agenda	_____
Presenters	_____
Finance	_____
Results Plan summary	_____
Flip chart	_____
Samples or pictures	_____
Resumes	_____
Research recap	_____
Tone of voice	_____

Humor/serious   _____

Next three steps   _____

Getting to yes!   _____

Convincing closing _____

Tough questions   _____

Answers   _____

Use these steps and you will have a business plan presentation for finance people that is far above average. Past patterns indicate that this approach is very likely to help you reach your capital generating objectives.

30

Winning Special People

To gain believability, make an admission.

— C. Scott

The success of your plan depends on acceptance of it and support for it by various key players. Among these are your immediate management team (such as your sales, finance, or production managers) and several other vital people (such as your banker and your owners or stockholders). If just one of these groups is in strong disagreement, you have a serious problem and the plan can fail. If all strongly support the plan, it is more likely to succeed.

The purpose of this section is to discuss a few simple steps you can take to achieve this consensus and support. Then we'll look at a demonstration of such an approach and finally a plans outline that will help you do the same.

Here we discuss how to design your written business plan, and how to fill out the various forms provided here so that they generate enthusiastic endorsement. We will discuss some general guidelines or viewpoints usually held by the immediate team and other key people. We'll look at their desire to be respected and accepted. We'll also review the specific interests of key people, such as finance or production managers. Then we'll look at a demonstration chart showing how one company recognized these wants, needs, hopes, fears, and personal goals and then did something about them. They covered each of these, realized, recognized, and resolved them in the plan and so generated strong, even enthusiastic support for the program by all key groups. We conclude with a similar (but blank) form for you to use in your company.

Recognize that you have two key groups, your immediate team and other key people.

Your immediate team is usually made up of your management, finance, sales, technical, production, and support staff.

Your other key people are usually your board of directors, shareholders, bankers, and outside support groups like your advertising agency, lawyer, and sometimes even your suppliers and dealers or distributors.

GUIDELINES

- Each of these people or groups speaks a slightly different language and has different viewpoints, problems, worries, and different goals.

- Learn these, as best you can. You can't speak their language if you have never heard it.

- Write the plan with the help of people who must often talk in other people's terms (such as general managers and sales, marketing and advertising specialists).

- Know what you want to accomplish (acceptance and support), and show how the plan accomplishes the goals of others.

- Perhaps the greatest generator of support for a plan is simply respect for other people's opinions. This is best shown by sharing the plan with them, asking their opinions and suggestions, and by accommodating their ideas, even if only in a small way. Then they become involved they become a personal part of the plan. It becomes *their* plan.

- The management team mainly wants to know that they are involved, that they have an effective input, and that people are listening to them. They also wish to see that their area is given fair and reasonable goals and roles.

- More specifically, management wants to avoid errors, loss and waste; to make good use of resources; and to show a good profit and ROI.

- Finance people want to be sure there is good cost control, as well as a realistic profit and loss, balance sheet, and cash-flow plan.

- Marketing wants to know that the goods and services are properly designed for maximum acceptability by the customer, and that marketing has the ability to communicate this.

- Production wants to know that the product and service design is such that it can be efficiently produced with proper quantity, quality, schedules, and cost control.

- The board of directors wants to be sure that the program guards the general health and reputation of the company, generating profits and dividends for the shareholders (which often includes the board members).

- Shareholders are primarily concerned with profits for dividend, as well as the firm's reputation in the investor community, leading to increased demand for the stock.

- The banker worries about repayment and net worth as a form of collateral behind the loan. He or she wants to see safety, capital conservation, and realistic income projections (gross and net). If he sees a good, realistic, and reachable loan repayment schedule, he worries less.

- In appealing to all, the plan should be sensible and thorough. It should begin by building on sound facts, review resources, and then agree upon objectives and strategic steps for reaching these goals. Use the 5 W's,

SWOT, 8 P's and KRA. Both immediate team members and other key groups respond well to such a plan. They can understand it, visualize it, and support it.

● The plan should recognize, acknowledge, and repeat the major concerns and goals of key groups. It should show how these are accommodated, resolved, and reached.

MATCHING INDIVIDUAL INTERESTS TO PLANNING

Group	Interests, Viewpoints, Fears, and Goals	How to Win Support
Management	Wants close coordination, input, watch goals and check all departments and ROI.	Directs the planning. Sets up forms, meeting, and plan preparation and presentation.
Finance	Wants to be involved. Cost control, profit and loss.	Helps prepare forecasts—profit and loss, cash flow chart.
Marketing	Saleable product. Ability to communicate ideas.	Helps test product/service. Designs market program.
Production	Consulted, product design, quality, quantity, time.	Helps design product, schedule quantities. Control quality.
Board of Directors	Informed. Involved. Guard company image/profit.	Explain plan. Ask input. Take advice. Plan profit.
Shareholders	Concerned with profits and company image/stock.	Show image and profit plan.
All	Want safety, progress for individual and company	Show sound sound, tested, progressive, thorough.

Here's a practical project form for you to use to win support from key groups.

WINNING SUPPORT FROM KEY GROUPS

Group	Interests, Viewpoints, Fears, and Goals	How to Win Support
Management	_____ _____	_____ _____
Finance	_____ _____	_____ _____
Marketing	_____ _____	_____ _____
Production	_____ _____	_____ _____
Board of Directors	_____ _____	_____ _____
Shareholders	_____ _____	_____ _____
All	_____ _____	_____ _____

Use these procedures, understand the wants and needs of your various groups, and construct your plan to fill those interests, and you are very likely to generate strong support.

Bibliography

Here is a list of books and shorter items that can help you. If you wish to get more information on one of various fields, please consider using one of the sources.

<u>FREE or low cost</u>

(The following are pamphlets or one-pagers. For SBAPublications, an order list is available at your local SBA Office or call 1-800-368-5855)

GENERAL MANAGEMENT

Developing A Strategic Business Plan. Policastro, Michael L. 1987. $1. The Travelers & SBA.

Planning and Goal Setting for Small Business. Pelissier, Raymond F. 1968. $.50. International Consulting Associates & SBA.

Business Plan for Retailers. SBA, 1988. $1.00.

Business Plan for Small Service Firms. SBA. $.50.

Business Plan for Small Manufacturers. SBA. $1.00.

How to Buy or Sell A Business. SBA. $1.00.

How to Really Start Your Own Business. SBA and Inc. Magazine. Booklet $1.00. Video Tape, $42.45.

FINANCIAL ANALYSIS

Basic Budgets for Profit Planning. SBA. $.50.

Sound Cash Management and Borrowing. SBA. $.50.

A Venture Capital Primer for Small Businesses. SBA. $.50.

MARKETING

Marketing for the Small Business: An Overview. SBA. $1.00.

Marketing Checklist for Small Retailers. SBA. $1.00.

Advertising. SBA. $1.00.

PERSONNEL MANAGEMENT

Checklist for Developing a Training Program. SBA. $.50.

Employees: How to Find and Pay Them. SBA. $1.00.

PRODUCTION/NEW PRODUCTS/IDEAS

Can You Make Money with Your Idea or Invention? SBA. $.50.

Techniques for Productivity Improvement. SBA. $1.00.

Introduction to Patents. SBA. $.50.

SBA 8(a) Business Plan Form 1010C(10-89); 33 Pages of Forms. SBA. Free.

<u>REGULAR PRICED BOOKS - Mostly full sized.</u>

GENERAL MANAGEMENT

Your Team Of Tigers. Rice, Craig S. 1982. American Management Association.

Power Secrets Of Managing People. Rice, Craig S. 1980. Prentice-Hall.

Small Business Management. Siropolis, Nicholas C. 1986. Houghton Mifflin.

Small Business Management Fundamentals. Steinhoff, Dan and Burgess, John F. 1986. McGraw-Hill.

Retail Management: A Strategic Approach. 3rd Ed., Berman, Barr and Evans, Joel R. 1986. MacMillian Publishing Co.

Buying and Selling a Business. Coltman, Michael M. 1983. ISC Press.

Complete Guide to Buying and Selling a Business. Goldstein, Arnold S. 1983. Ronald Press.

How to Generate New, Original, Moneymaking Ideas. Mulville, Dean R. 1980. American Classical College Press.

Small Business Opportunities. Chapman, A.C. 1984. Prentice-Hall.

Decision Making for Small Business Management. Young, Jerrald F. 1982. Krieger.

New Venture Creation: A Guide to Small Business Development. Timmons, Jeffrey A. 1985. Irwin.

MARKETING

Marketing Without a Marketing Budget. Rice, Craig S. 1989. Bob Adams, Inc.

Marketing Planning Strategies. Rice, Craig S. 1984. Dartnell.

Promotional Strategy. 5th Ed., Engel, James F., Warshaw, Martin R. and Kinnear, Thomas C. 1983. Richard D. Irwin, Inc.

Promotion: Products, Service and Ideas. 2nd Ed., Kincaid, William M. 1985. Charles E. Merrill Publishing Co.

Profitable Methods for Small Business Advertising. Gray, Ernest E. 1984. Ronald Press.

Merchandising Mathematics for Retailing. Easterling, Cynthia R., Flottman, Ellen and Jernigan, Marian H. 1984. John Wiley & Sons.

Practical Marketing for Your Small Retail Business. Brannen, William H. 1981. John Wiley & Sons.

Advertising and Public Relations for Small Business. Bellavance, Diane. 1982. BBA Books.

Advertising for The Small Business. Dean, Sandra L. 1980. Self Counsel Press.

Handbook for Small Business Advertising. Anthony, Michael. 1981. Addison-Wesley.

Low Cost Market Research: Guide for Small Business. Gorton, Keith and Carr, Isobel. 1983. Wiley.

Profitable Sales Management & Marketing for a Growing Business. Calvin, Robert J. 1984. Van Nostrand Reinhold.

FINANCE AND ACCOUNTING

Accounting, Finance and Taxation: A Basic Guide for Small Business. Baker, C. Richard and Hayes, Rick S. 1980. CBI Publishers.

Practical Accounting for Small Business. Kirsner, Laura T. 1983. Van Nostrand Reinhold.

Assisting Small Business Clients in Obtaining Funds. 1982. American Institute of CPAs.

How to Finance Your Small Business with Government Money: SBA and Other Loans. 2nd Ed. Hayes, Rick S. and Howell, John C. 1983. Ronald Press.

Insider's Guide to Small Business Resources. Gumpert, David E., and Timmons, Jeffrey. 1982. Doubleday.

Business Capital Sources. 2nd Ed., Hicks, Tyler G. 1983. International Wealth.

Financial Tools for Small Business. Carey, Omer and Olson, Dean. 1983. Reston.

How to Borrow Money from a Bank. Alexander, Don H. 1983. DHA Associates.

Collection Techniques for the Small Business. Paulsen, Timothy R. 1984. ISC Press.

Small Business Computers for the First-time Users. Beaman, I.R. 1983. International Publications Service.

Profit-line Management: Managing a Growing Business Successfully. Holtz, Herman R. 1981. AMACOM.

Profit Secrets for Small Business. Stevens, Mark. 1983. Reston.

PRODUCTION

Operations Management: Productivity and Quality. 2nd Ed., Schonberger, Richard. 1985. Business Publications.

Productivity Improvement: A Guide for Small Business. Gregerman, Ira B. 1984. Van Nostrand Reinhold.

PERSONNEL MANAGEMENT

People Par Excellence. Rice, Craig S. 1984. American Management Association.

Getting Good People and Keeping Them. Rice, Craig S. 1982. American Management Associations.

Successful Small Business Management, 4th Ed., Tate, Curtis E., Meggison, Leon C. Scott, Charles R., and Trueblood, Gayle R. 1985. Business Publications, Inc.

Practical Personnel Policies for the Small Business. Cohn, Theodore and Lindberg, Roy A. 1983. CBI Publishing.

Staffing a Small Business: Hiring, Compensating & Evaluating Worthington, Anita E, Worthington, E. Robert. 1985. Oasis.

EXPORTING

How to Prepare and Process Export-import Documents: A Fully Illustrated Guide. Hicks, Tyler G. 1983. International Wealth Press.

PENSIONS

Successful Pension Design for the Small to Medium Size Business. Slimmon, Robert F. 1980. Institute for Business Planning.

PURCHASING

Effective Purchasing and Inventory Control for Small Business. Dollar, William E. 1983. CBI Publishers.

SECURITY

Security for Small Business. Berger, David. 1981. Butterworth.

PERSONAL and TIME

Have You Got What It Takes? Mancuso, Joseph R. 1982. Prentice-Hall.

The Time Manager. Edwards, Paul and Sara. 1983. Home Enterprises Unlimited.

TRADE/PROFESSIONAL ASSOCIATIONS

American Management Association. 135 West 50th St., New York NY 10020.

American Marketing Association. 250 S. Wacker Dr., Chicago IL 60606.

American Federation of Small Businesses. 407 So. Dearborn, Chicago IL 60608.

Council of Smaller Enterprises. 690 Union Commerce Building, Cleveland OH 44115.

National Association for Public Continuing and Adult Education. 1201 16th NW, Washington DC 20036.

Center for Entrepreneurial Management. 83 Spring St., New York NY 10012.

National Business League. 4324 Georgia Ave. NW, Washington DC 20005.

National Federation Of Independent Business. 150 West 20th Ave., San Mateo CA 94403.

National Small Business Association. 1604 K St. NW, Washington DC 20006.

Small Business Foundation Of America. 69 Hickory Dr., Waltham MA 02154.

United Federation Of Small Business. 4817 Palm Ave, #A, La Mesa CA 92041.